Ch'angdŏkkung Palace
Sŏnggyun-gwan Univ
Seoul Univ Hospital
Ch'anggyŏnggung Palace
YULGOK-RO
#4 SUBWAY
Ewha Univ Hospital
KAIST
Ch'ŏngnyangni Station
Royal Shrine
Pagoda Park
East Gate
CHONG-RO
#1 SUBWAY
Donga Ilbo
The Korea Development Bank
Medical Center
Tongdaemun Stadium
CH'ŎNGGYECH'ŎN-RO
Chohŭng Bank
#3 SUBWAY
ŬLCHI-RO
#2 SUBWAY
Catholic Church
Savoy Hotel
TOEGYE-RO
Sofitel Ambassador
Sejong Hotel
Chinese Embassy
Korea House
Changch'ung Stadium
Hanyang Univ Hospital
Hanyang Univ
Int'l Cultural Society of Korea
Astoria Hotel
Tongguk Univ
Hotel Shilla
Namsan Park
#1 TUNNEL
#2 TUNNEL
#3 TUNNEL
National Theater
Sheraton Walker Hill
Namsan Pavilion
Tower Hotel
Seoul Tower
Retreat Center
German Cultural Center
Hyatt Regency Seoul
SŎNGSU BRIDGE
Konkuk Univ
It'aewon Village
Hannam Foreigner's Village
UN Village
TONGHO BRIDGE
Sunch'ŏnhyang Hospital
Tan-guk Univ
YŎNGDONG BRIDGE
Moslem Temple
Sports Park
HANNAM BRIDGE
HAN RIVER
OLYMPIC TAERO
#3 SUBWAY
South Post Golf Club
TONGJAK BRIDGE
PANP'O BRIDGE
Express Bus Terminal
Palace Hotel

# LET'S TALK
# in
# KOREAN

# LET'S TALK in KOREAN

**Second Revised Edition**

*by*
Pong Kook Lee
Chi Sik Ryu

HOLLYM
Elizabeth, NJ · Seoul

**Let's Talk in Korea**



First published in 1979
Revised edition, 1982
Tenth printing, 1998
Second Revised edition, 1999
Second printing, 2001
by Hollym International Corp.
18 Donald Place, Elizabeth, NJ 07208, USA
Phone:(908)353-1655 Fax:(908)353-0255
http://www.hollym.com

Published simultaneously in Korea
by Hollym Corporation; Publishers
13-13 Kwanchol-dong, Chongno-gu, Seoul 110-111, Korea
Phone: (02)735-7551~4 Fax: (02)730-5149, 8192
http://www.hollym.co.kr

ISBN: 0-930878-10-8
Library of Congress Catalog Card Number: 78-72953

*Printed in Korea*

# PREFACE

This is a pocket-book version of our earlier work, "Easy Way To KOREAN CONVERSATION," but amply revised and supplemented to better meet the actual needs of talking to Koreans in various situations.

Part I deals with the basic words and expressions which are most frequently used and can be easily applied. Part II covers practically all the topics that may interest learners.

It would be good to have helpful friends beside you in learning the dialogues and expressions used in this book, and to use the material as a basis for discussions. There are always many ways to express relatively simple things, and you will find that we Koreans do not agree among ourselves from time to time on the spelling of words, and particularly the way Korean letters should be romanized. We have followed the Ministry of Education System with minor revisions and tried to make the transcription appear and sound as natural as possible.

We hope this small book may be a good stepping stone for you to go on to more advanced conversations and readings.

*Pong Kook Lee*

*Chi Sik Ryu*

# CONTENTS

## PART III VOCABULARIES

**APPENDIX I**



**APPENDIX II**

*TO HELP YOU UNDERSTAND KOREAN ALPHABET AND SOME WRITINGS IN KOREAN*

# PART I

# BASIC WORDS AND SENTENCES

# I. GREETINGS AND LEAVE TAKINGS

1. Good morning.
   Good afternoon.
   Good evening.

2. How do you do?
   How are you?

3. I'm fine, thank you.
   Very well, thank you.

---

(1) Most Western greetings including "Hello" could be expressed by (annyŏnghashimnikka?)(안녕하십니까?) or by its short form (annyŏnghaseyo?)(안녕하세요?).

(2) Koreans usually repeat (annyŏnghahimnikka?) for an answer, but if one wishes to apply Western ways of answering, he may say,

ne, chossŭmnida, komapsŭmnida.
네, 좋 습니다, 고 맙 습 니다.

# I. 인　　사

1. Annyŏnghashimnikka?[1]
   안 녕 하 십 니 까?

2. Annyŏnghashimnikka?
   안 녕 하 십 니 까?

3. Ne, chossŭmnida, komapsŭmnida.[2]
   네, 좋 습 니다, 고 맙 습 니다.

---

or simply, as the following:

(chossŭmnida, komapsŭmnida.)
좋 습 니다, 고 맙 습 니다.

((ne) chossŭmnida.)
네 좋 습 니다.

((ne) komapsŭmnida.)
네 고 맙 습 니다.

The use of (ne)(네) here is simply a Korean cultural pattern. See page 24 for its proper affirmative function.

4. I'm glad to see you.

5. Hello, Mr. Kim.

6. Hello, Miss Lee.

7. Good-bye.

8. Good night.

9. I'll see you later.

   I hope to see you again.

10. I'll see you soon.

11. Have a good time.

12. Have a nice trip.
    Bon voyage.

13. Good luck, Mrs. Yu.

14. Remember me to President Oh.

4. Manna poeŏ pan-gapsŭmnida.
만 나 뵈 어 반 갑 습 니다.
5. Kim sŏnsaengnim, annyŏnghashimnikka?
김 선 생 님, 안 녕 하 십 니 까?
6. I yang, annyŏnghashimnikka?
이 양, 안 녕 하 십 니 까?
7. Annyŏnghi kashipshio.
안 녕 히 가 십 시오.
Annyŏnghi kyeshipshio.
안 녕 히 계 십 시오.
8. Annyŏnghi chumushipshio.
안 녕 히 주 무 십 시오.
9. Tto poepkessŭmnida.
또 뵙 겠 습 니 다.

10. Kot poepkessŭmnida.
곧 뵙 겠 습 니다.
11. Chŭlgŏpke chinaeshipshio.
즐 겁 게 지 내 십 시오.
12. Chŭlgŏun yŏhaengŭl haseyo.
즐 거운 여 행 을 하세요.

13. Yu yŏsanim, haeng-unŭl pimnida.
유 여사 님, 행 운을 빕 니다.
14. O sajangnimkke anbu chŏnhae chuseyo.
오 사 장 님 께 안부 전 해 주 세요.

# II. THANKS AND APOLOGIES

1. Thanks.
   Thank you.
2. Thank you very much.
3. Don't mention it.
   Not at all.
   You are welcome.
4. I'm sorry.
5. Excuse me.
6. Pardon me.
7. Forgive me.
   I beg your pardon.
8. I beg your pardon?
9. I must apologize.
10. It's nothing.

# II. 감사와 사과

1. Komapsŭmnida.
   고 맙 습 니다.

2. Taedanhi komapsŭmnida.
   대 단히 고 맙 습 니다.
3. Ch'ŏnmanŭi malssŭmimnida.
   천 만의 말 씀 입니다.

4. Mianhamnida.
   미안 합 니다.
5. Shillyehamnida.
   실 례 합 니다.
6. Choesonghamnida.
   죄 송 합 니다.
7. Yongsŏhashipshio.
   용 서하 십 시오.

8. Tashi malssŭmhae chushigessŭmnikka?
   다시 말 씀 해 주 시겠 습 니 까?
9. Yongsŏrŭl pirŏyagessŭmnida.
   용 서를 빌어야겠 습 니다.
10. Kwaench'anssŭmnida.
    괜 찮 습 니다.

# III. IMPERATIVES

1. Please come in.
2. Sit down, please.
   Have a seat, please.
3. Let's go out.
4. Let's start now.
5. Let's look around.
6. Drop in any time.
7. Call me up sometime.
8. Fill in this card.
9. Write your name here.
10. Sign your name here.

---

(1), (2) Sŏngham(성함) is an honorific form of sŏngmyŏng(성명) which means the family name and the given name. Sŏmyŏng means "signing of name."

# III. 명 령

1. Ŏsŏ tŭrŏoshipshio.
   어서 들어오십 시오.
2. Anjŭshipshio.
   앉으십 시오.
3. Nagapshida.
   나 갑 시 다.
4. Chigŭm ttŏnapshida.
   지 금 떠 납 시 다.
5. Tullŏbopshida.
   둘 러 봅 시 다.
6. Amuttaena tŭllŭseyo.
   아무 때 나 들르세요.
7. Ŏnje hanbŏn chŏnhwahaseyo.
   언 제 한 번 전 화 하 세 요.
8. I k'adŭe kiip'ashipshio.
   이 카드에 기입하 십 시오.
9. Yŏgie sŏnghamŭl(1) ssŭshipshio.
   여 기에 성 함 을 쓰 십 시 오.
10. Yŏgie sŏmyŏnghashipshio.(2)
    여기에 서 명 하 십 시오.

---

All those three words are from Chinese, but original Korean word for "name" is irŭm(이름).

11. Wait for me in the lobby.

12. Just a moment, please.

Seoul Station

11. Robiesŏ kidaryŏ chushipshio.
    로비에서기다려 주십시오.
12. Chamkkanman kidaryŏ chushipshio.
    잠깐만 기다려 주십시오.

# IV. QUESTIONS

1. Are you Professor Kang?

2. Yes, I am.

3. Is this Dr. Ko's office?

4. Yes, it is.

5. Is she Mrs. Chang?

6. No, she is not.

7. She is Mrs. Kwon.

8. Can you speak English?

9. Yes, a little.

10. Do you know Miss Song?

---

(1) (Ye) (예) is standard, but (ne) (네) is quite often used, and sometimes (nye) (녜) is also heard.

(2) For most affirmative answers it is quite frequently used.

# IV. 묻는 말

1. Kang kyosunimishimnikka?
   강 교수님이십 니까?
2. Ne,[1] kŭrŏssŭmnida.[2]
   네, 그렇 습 니다.
3. Yŏgiga Ko paksanimŭi samushirimnikka?
   여기가 고 박사님의 사무 실입니까?
4. Ne, kŭrŏssŭmnida.
   네, 그렇 습 니다.
5. Chŏbuni Chang yŏsaimnikka?
   저 분이 장 여사입니까?
6. Animnida.[3]
   아닙 니다.
7. Kwŏn yŏsaimnida.
   권 여사입니다.
8. Yŏng-ŏrŭl hashimnikka?
   영 어를 하 십 니까?
9. Ne, chom hamnida.
   네, 좀 합 니다.
10. Misŭ Song-ŭl aseyo?
    미스 송 을아세요?

---

to mean, "You are right," or "That is right."

(3) This means "That is not so."

11. Yes, I do.

12. Shall we go now?

13. Yes, let's go.

14. Will you do me a favor?

15. With pleasure.

16. May I come in?

17. Yes, of course.

18. Must you leave now?

19. Yes, I must.

20. What is your name?

21. My name is Chon Myong Su.

22. Who is that gentleman?

---

(4) This is a literal translation.
(5) An other expression toemnikka(됩니까) is also possible.
(6) See note (1) page 20.
(7) (chŏŭi)(저의) may be contracted to (che)(제).

11. Ne, amnida.
네, 압니다.
12. Chigŭm kalkkayo?
지금 갈까요?
13. Ne, kapshida.
네, 갑시다.
14. Put'agŭl tŭrŏ chushigessŭmnikka?
부탁을 들어 주시겠습니까?
15. Ne, kikkŏi hae tŭrijiyo.(4)
네, 기꺼이 해 드리지요.
16. Tŭrŏgado chossŭmnikka?
들어가도 좋습니까?
17. Ne, mullonijiyo.
네, 물론이지요.
18. Chigŭm kkok ttŏnaya hamnikka? (5)
지금 꼭 떠나야 합니까?
19. Ne, ttŏnaya hamnida.
네, 떠나야 합니다.
20. Sŏnghami [irŭmi] muŏshimnikka? (6)
성함이[이름이] 무엇입니까?
21. Chŏŭi(7) irŭmŭn Chŏn Myŏngsuimnida.
저의 이름은 전 명수입니다.
22. Chŏbunŭn(8) nuguimnikka?
저 분은 누구입니까?

(8) Literally, gentleman in Korean is (shinsa)(신사) but this is rarely used in conversation. (Pun)(분) is an honorific form of man or person. Therefore it be may well used for "gentleman" in English.

23. He is our vice-president.

24. Which do you like?

25. I like this one.

26. Whose car is this?

27. It is mine.

28. Who(m) do you want to see?

29. I want to meet Mr. Nam.

30. Where is the company?

31. It is just over there.

32. When shall we meet?

33. Let's meet tomorrow.

34. How can I get there?

35. You can get there by subway.

23. Uri pusajangimnida.
우리부사 장 입니다.
24. Ŏnŭ kŏsŭl choahashimnikka?
어느 것을 좋아하 십 니까?
25. Igŏshi chossŭmnida.(Maŭme tŭmnida.)
이것이 좋 습 니다. (마 음에 듭 니다.)
26. Igŏsŭn nuguŭi ch'aimnikka?
이것은 누구의 차 입니 까?
27. Che ch'aimnida.
제 차 입니다.
28. Nugurŭl mannashiryŏmnikka?
누 구를 만 나 시 렵 니 까?
29. Nam sŏnsaengnimŭl mannago shipsŭmnida.
남 선 생 님 을 만 나고 싶 습 니다.
30. Kŭ hoesanŭn ŏdie issŭmnikka?
그 회 사 는 어디에 있습니까?
31. Paro chŏgie issŭmnida.
바로 저기에 있습니다.
32. Ŏnje mannalkkayo?
언제 만 날 까 요?
33. Naeil mannapshida.
내 일 만 납 시다.
34. Kŭ kose ŏttŏk'e kal su issŭmnikka?
그 곳에 어떻게 갈 수있 습 니 까?
35. Chihach'ŏllo kal su issŭmnida.
지 하 철 로 갈 수있 습 니다.

36. How much is this?

37. It is 1,000 won.

38. How many do you want?

39. I want two.

40. How long will you stay?

41. I'll stay for three weeks.

36. Igŏsŭn ŏlmaimnikka?
이것은 얼마 입니 까?
37. Ch'ŏnwŏnimnida.
천 원 입니다.
38. Myŏt kaerŭl wŏnhashimnikka?
몇 개를 원하십 니까?
39. Tu kaerŭl wŏnhamnida.
두 개를 원 합 니다.
40. Ŏlma tongan mŏmurŭshigessŭmnikka?
얼마 동안 머무르시겠 습 니까?
41. Sam chuil tongan mŏmurŭgessŭmnida.
삼 주일 동안 머무르겠 습 니다.

Subway Station

# V. TIME

1. What time is it?
2. It is one o'clock.
3. It is two-thirty.
4. It is half past three.
5. It is a quarter to four.
6. It's a quarter past five.
7. It's six a.m.
8. It's seven p.m.

# V. 시 간

1. Myŏt shiimnikka?
   몇 시 입니까?
2. Hanshiimnida.
   한 시 입니다.
3. Tushi samshippunimnida.
   두 시 삼 십 분 입니다.
4. Seshi panimnida.
   세 시 반 입니다.
5. Neshi shibobun chŏnimnida.
   네 시 십 오분 전 입니다.
6. Tasŏssi shibobunimnida.
   다섯 시 십 오분 입니다.
7. Ojŏn yŏsŏssiimnida.
   오전 여섯 시 입니다.
8. Ohu ilgopshiimnida.
   오후 일곱 시 입니다.

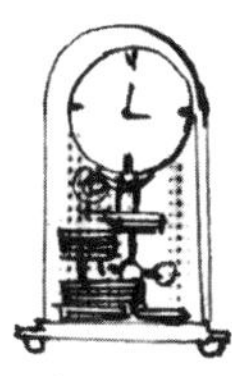

# VI. CALENDAR

1. What day is it today?

2. Today is Monday.

3. It is January 3rd.

4. It is Tuesday, February 5th.

5. What season do you like best?

6. I like spring best.

# VI. 달 력

1. Onŭrŭn myŏch'irimnikka?
   오늘은 며 칠 입니까?
   or,
   Onŭrŭn musŭn yoirimnikka?
   오늘은 무 슨 요일입니까?
2. Onŭrŭn wŏryoirimnida.
   오늘은 월 요일입니다.
3. Onŭrŭn irwŏl samirimnida.
   오늘은 일월 삼 일입니다.
4. Onŭrŭn iwŏl oil hwayoirimnida.
   오늘은 이월 오일 화 요일입니다.
5. Ŏnŭ kyejŏrŭl kajang choahashimnikka?
   어느 계절을 가장 좋아하 십 니까?
6. Pomŭl kajang choahamnida.
   봄을 가장 좋아합 니다.

# PART II

# DAILY CONVERSATION

# I. INTRODUCTIONS

## ☐ Useful Expressions

1. I'll introduce you to Mr. Lee.
2. Allow me to introduce my friends.
3. Mr. Williams, this is my friend Mr. Kang.
4. I'm glad to meet you.
5. May I introduce Mr. Smith, our manager?
6. I would like you to meet my wife.
7. Would you like to be introduced to him?
8. I should like to be introduced to Miss Yang.
9. Do you have a calling card?
10. Excuse me, I don't have a calling card.
11. It is nice to meet you.

# I. 소 개

## □ 많이 쓰는 표현

1. I sŏnsaengnimŭl sogaehagessŭmnida.
   이 선생님을 소개하겠습니다.
2. Che ch'in-gurŭl sogaehagessŭmnida.
   제 친구를 소개하겠습니다.
3. Williŏmjŭ ssi, che ch'in-gu misŭt'ŏ Kangimnida.
   윌리엄즈 씨, 제 친구 미스터 강입니다.
4. Manna poeŏ pan-gapsŭmnida.
   만나 뵈어 반갑습니다.
5. Chŏŭi chibaein Sŭmidŭ ssirŭl sogaehae tŭrilkka-yo?
   저의 지배인 스미드 씨를 소개해 드릴까요?
6. Che anaeimnida. 제 아내입니다.
7. Kŭ[Chŏ]bunege (tangshinŭl) sogaehae tŭrilkka-yo?
   그[저]분에게 (당신을) 소개해 드릴까요?
8. Misŭ Yang-ege sogaehae chushigi paramnida.
   미스 양에게 소개해 주시기 바랍니다.
9. Myŏnghamŭl kajigo kyeshimnikka?
   명함을 가지고 계십니까?
10. Mianhamnida. Myŏnghami ŏpsŭmnida.
    미안합니다. 명함이 없습니다
11. Manna poeŏ kippŭmnida.
    만나 뵈어 기쁩니다.

## 12. I hope to meet you again sometime.

### 1. At the Airport

*(Mr. Smith arrives at Inch'ŏn International Airport from the United States.)*

**Mr. Kim :** Welcome, Mr. Smith. How are you?

**Mr. Smith :** Fine. And you?

**Mr. Kim :** I'm fine, too.

Mr. Smith, this is Mr. Kang, manager of our company.

**Mr. Smith :** How do you do, Mr. Kang? I'm glad to meet you.

**Mr. Kang :** How do you do, Mr. Smith? Welcome to Korea.

### 2. On the Street

*(Mr. Johnson is a tourist from America and is visiting*

12. (Ŏnje) Tashi poepki paramnida.
(언제) 다시 뵙기 바랍니다.

## 1. 공항에서

(스미드 씨는 미국을 떠나 지금 인천국제공항에 도착했다.)

K : Ŏsŏ oshipshio, Sŭmidŭ ssi.
Annyŏnghashimnikka?
어서 오십시오, 스미드 씨.
안녕하십니까?

S : Ne. (chossŭmnida.) Annyŏnghashimnikka?
네. (좋습니다.) 안녕하십니까?

K : Ne. (chossŭmnida.) Sŭmidŭ ssi, chŏhŭi hoesa chibaein misŭt'ŏ Kangimnida.
네. (좋습니다.) 스미드 씨. 저희 회사 지배인 미스터 강입니다.

S : Annyŏnghashimnikka, misŭt'ŏ Kang?
Manna poeŏ pan-gapsŭmnida.
안녕하십니까, 미스터 강?
만나 뵈어 반갑습니다.

K : Annyŏnghashimnikka, misŭt'ŏ Sŭmidŭ? Han-guge oshin kŏsŭl hwanyŏnghamnida.
안녕하십니까, 미스터 스미드? 한국에 오신 것을 환영합니다.

## 2. 거리에서

(존슨 씨는 미국에서 온 관광객이다. 그는 서울에 와서 그

*Seoul with his friend Mr. Song. They come across Mr. Namgung, Mr. Song's friend.)*

**Mr. Namgung :** Hello, Mr. Song.

**Mr. Song :** Oh, Hello, Mr. Namgung.

Mr. Johnson, this is my friend Mr. Namgung.

He works for the Chase Manhattan Bank here.

**Mr. Namgung :** How do you do, Mr. Johnson?

I'm glad to meet you.

**Mr. Johnson :** How do you do, Mr. Namgung?

**Mr. Song :** Mr. Johnson is visiting our country.

He is from St. Louis where my brother is living.

**Mr. Namgung :** Oh, is that so? I hope you will enjoy your stay here.

의 친구 Mr. 송을 만났다. 그들은 함께 Mr. 송의 친구 Mr. 남궁을 우연히 만난다.)

**N** : Annyŏnghaseyo, misŭt'ŏ Song.
안녕하세요, 미스터 송.

**S** : Ah, annyŏnghaseyo, misŭt'ŏ Namgung.
Chonsŭn ssi, che ch'in-gu misŭt'ŏ Namgung-imnida. Ibunŭn i kot Ch'eisŭ Maenhaet'ŏn ŭnhaengesŏ irhago kyeshimnida.
아, 안녕하세요, 미스터 남궁.
존슨 씨, 제 친구 미스터 남궁입니다.
이분은 이 곳 체이스 맨해턴 은행에서 일하고 계십니다.

**N** : Annyŏnghashimnikka, Chonsŭn ssi?
Manna poeŏ pan-gapsŭmnida.
안녕하십니까, 존슨 씨?
만나 뵈어 반갑습니다.

**J** : Annyŏnghashimnikka, Namgungssi?
안녕하십니까, 남궁씨?

**S** : Chonsŭn ssinŭn uri nararŭl pangmun chung-imnida.
Che hyŏngnimi sanŭn Seint'ŭruisŭesŏ osyŏssŭmnida.
존슨 씨는 우리 나라를 방문 중입니다.
제 형님이 사는 세인트루이스에서 오셨습니다.

**N** : Ah, kŭrŏssŭmnikka?
Yŏgi kyeshinŭn tongan mani chŭlgishigi paramnida.
아, 그렇습니까? 여기 계시는 동안 많이 즐기시기 바랍니다.

**Mr. Johnson** : Thank you.

**Mr. Namgung** : Well, I'll be on my way.

**Mr. Song & Mr. Johnson** : Good-bye.

**Mr. Namgung** : Good-bye.

### 3. In the Office

(*Mr. Lee ushers Mr. Smith into Mr. Kim's office.*)

**Mr. Lee** : Good afternoon, Mr. Kim. May I introduce Mr. Smith, a college friend of mine from New York. Dick, this is Mr. Kim, head of our business department.

**Mr. Smith** : How do you do, Mr. Kim?

**Mr. Kim** : How do you do, Mr. Smith?
I'm glad to meet you.
Please have a seat.

Mr. Lee has told me a lot about you.

**Mr. Smith** : Thank you.

J : Komapsŭmnida.
고맙습니다.

N: Kŭrŏm, kaboaya hagessŭmnida.
그럼, 가보아야 하겠습니다.

S.J: Annyŏnghi kashipshio.
안녕히 가십시오.

N : Annyŏnghi kashipshio.
안녕히 가십시오.

## 3. 사무실에서

(Mr. 리의 안내로 스미드 씨는 Mr. 김의 사무실로 들어왔다.)

L : Annyŏnghashimnikka, misŭt'ŏ Kim. Nyuyok'ŭesŏ on (che) taehak tongch'ang Sŭmidŭ ssirŭl sogaedŭrigessŭmnida. Tik, uri yŏngŏppu Kim pujangimnida.
안녕하십니까, 미스터 김. 뉴요크에서 온 (제) 대학 동창 스미드 씨를 소개해 드리겠습니다. 딕, 우리 영업부 김 부장입니다.

S : Annyŏnghashimnikka, misŭt'ŏ Kim?
안녕하십니까, 미스터 김?

K : Annyŏnghashimnikka, Sŭmidŭ ssi? Manna poeŏ pan-gapsŭmnida. Ŏsŏ anjŭshipshio. Misŭt'ŏ Riro-but'ŏ malssŭm mani tŭrŏssŭmnida.
안녕하십니까, 스미드 씨? 만나 뵈어 반갑습니다. 어서 앉으십시오. 미스터 리로부터 말씀 많이 들었습니다.

S : Komapsŭmnida.
고맙습니다.

**Mr. Kim :** How long have you been, Mr. Smith?

**Mr. Smith :** A little over a year. I've really enjoyed my stay here, thanks to Mr. Lee.

**Mr. Lee :** Mr. Smith is going back to the States next month, and wants to buy some Korean books.

**Mr. Kim :** That's wonderful. I think we can help you. Here's our catalogue.

**Mr. Smith :** Thank you very much.

That will be a great help.

4. Telephone

**Mr. Im :** Hello, Mr. Drake? How are you?

**Mr. Drake :** Fine, thank you, and you?

**Mr. Im :** I'm fine, too.

K : I kose ŏlmana kyesyŏssŭmnikka, Sŭmidŭ ssi?
이 곳에 얼마나 계셨습니까. 스미드 씨?

S : Illyŏn chogŭm nŏmŏssŭmnida. Misŭt'ŏ Ri tŏkpune yŏgi innŭn tongan chŏngmal chŭlgŏwŏssŭmnida.
일년 조금 넘었습니다. 미스터 리 덕분에 여기 있는 동안 정말 즐거웠습니다.

L : Sŭmidŭ ssinŭn taŭmtal Migugŭro toragashinŭnde, Han-guk ch'aegŭl chom saryŏgo hamnida.
스미드 씨는 다음달 미국으로 돌아가시는데, 한국 책을 좀 사려고 합니다.

K : Kŭgŏt ch'am chossŭmnida. Towa tŭrijiyo. Igŏshi uri (hoesa) k'at'allogŭimnida.
그것 참 좋습니다. 도와 드리지요. 이것이 우리 (회사) 카탈로그입니다.

S : Taedanhi komapsŭmnida. K'ŭn toumi toegessŭmnida.
대단히 고맙습니다. 큰 도움이 되겠습니다.

## 4. 전 화

I : Yŏboseyo, Tŭreik'ŭ ssiyeyo?
Annyŏnghaseyo?
여보세요, 드레이크 씨예요?
안녕하세요?

D : Ne, (chossŭmnida.) komapsŭmnida. Ŏttŏseyo?
네, (좋습니다.) 고맙습니다. 어떠세요?

I : Chŏdo chossŭmnida.

Well, my wife and I would like you to have dinner with us some time this weekend.

**Mr. Drake :** Oh, that would be very nice.

**Mr. Im :** How about this Saturday evening at 6 : 30?

**Mr. Drake :** Fine. Where shall I come?

**Mr. Im :** Do you think you can find our house aright?

**Mr. Drake :** Certainly. There'll be no problem.

**Mr. Im :** Then, we will be expecting you at 6 : 30 Saturday evening.

**Mr. Drake :** Thank you very much for inviting me. Good-bye.

**Mr. Im :** Good-bye.

Kŭrŏnde ibŏn chumare uriwa hamkke chŏnyŏgŭl haessŭmyŏn hanŭndeyo.
저도 좋습니다.
그런데 이번 주말에 우리와 함께 저녁을 했으면 하는데요.

D : Ah, kŭgŏt ch'am chossŭmnida.
아, 그것 참 좋습니다.

I : Ibŏn t'oyoil chŏnyŏk yŏsŏssi pani ŏttŏlkkayo?
이번 토요일 저녁 여섯시 반이 어떨까요?

D : Chossŭmnida. Ŏdiesŏ mannalkkayo?
좋습니다. 어디에서 만날까요?

I : Uri chibŭl paro ch'ajŭshil su itkessŏyo?
우리 집을 바로 찾으실 수 있겠어요?

D : Kŭrŏmyo. Munjeŏpsŭmnida.
그럼요. 문제 없습니다.

I : Kŭrŏm t'oyoil chŏnyŏk yŏsŏssi samshippune kidarigessŭmnida.
그럼 토요일 저녁 여섯시 삼십분에 기다리겠습니다.

D : Ch'odaehae chusyŏsŏ kamsahamnida.
Annyŏnghi kyeshipshio.
초대해 주셔서 감사합니다.
안녕히 계십시오.

I : Annyŏnghi kyeseyo.
안녕히 계세요.

# II. GETTING INFORMATIONS

## □ Useful Expressions

1. Is this the way to the Bank of Korea?
2. How far is it?
3. Is it far from here?
4. It's only a five minute walk.
5. How long does it take by car?
6. It will take an hour.
7. Go straight ahead and turn left.
8. Turn right and go around the fountain.
9. I am going in that direction.
10. It's a little too far to go on foot.
11. You had better take a taxi.

# II. 안 내

## □ 많이 쓰는 표현

1. I kiri Han-guk ŭnhaeng-ŭro kanŭn kirimnikka?
   이 길이 한국 은행으로 가는 길입니까?
2. Ŏlmana mŏmnikka?
   얼마나 멉니까?
3. Yŏgiesŏ mŏmnikka?
   여기에서 멉니까?
4. Obun chŏngdo kŏrŭmyŏn toemnida.
   오분 정도 걸으면 됩니다.
5. Chadongch'aronŭn ŏlmana kŏllimnikka?
   자동차로는 얼마나 걸립니까?
6. Han shigan kŏllimnida.
   한 시간 걸립니다.
7. Ttokparo kasŏ oentchogŭro toseyo.
   똑바로 가서 왼쪽으로 도세요.
8. Orŭntchogŭro torasŏ punsurŭl ttaragaseyo.
   오른쪽으로 돌아서 분수를 따라가세요.
9. Nanŭn kŭ tchogŭro kanŭn chungimnida.
   나는 그 쪽으로 가는 중입니다.
10. Kŏrŏsŏ kagienŭn chom mŏmnida.
    걸어서 가기에는 좀 멉니다.
11. T'aekshirŭl t'ashinŭn kŏshi choŭl kŏmnida.
    택시를 타시는 것이 좋을 겁니다.

12. Would you tell me when we get to Seoul?
13. I wish to go to this address.
14. Does this bus go to Seoul Station?
15. Could you tell me how to get to the bus terminal?

1. Chosun Hotel

**Mr. Duke :** Excuse me, but how do I get to the Chosun Hotel?

**Passer-by :** That's easy. Turn to the right at the corner there, and walk straight ahead one block. Then you will see the main entrance on your right.

**Mr. Duke :** Thank you very much.

**Passer-by :** You're welcome.

2. Toksu Palace

**Miss Wilson :** Can you tell me the way to

12. Ŏnje Sŏure tannŭnji aseyo?
언제 서울에 닿는지 아세요?
13. I chusoro ch'ajagaryŏmnida.
이 주소로 찾아가렵니다.
14. I pŏsŭga Sŏullyŏgŭro kamnikka?
이 버스가 서울역으로 갑니까?
15. Pŏsŭ chŏngnyujange ŏttŏk'e kanŭnji malssŭmhae chuseyo.
버스 정류장에 어떻게 가는지 말씀해 주세요.

## 1. 조선 호텔

**D** : Shillyehamnidaman Chosŏn hot'ere ŏttŏk'e kamnikka?
실례합니다만 조선 호텔에 어떻게 갑니까?

**P** : Aju shwiwŏyo. Chŏ mot'ungiesŏ orŭntchogŭro torasŏ kotchang han pŭllŏk kaseyo.
Kŭrŏmyŏn orŭntchoge chŏngmuni poimnida.
아주 쉬워요. 저 모퉁이에서 오른쪽으로 돌아서 곧장 한 블럭 가세요.
그러면 오른쪽에 정문이 보입니다.

**D** : Taedanhi kamsahamnida.
대단히 감사합니다.

**P** : Ch'onmaneyo.
천만에요.

## 2. 덕 수 궁

**W** : Tŏksugung kanŭn kirŭl karŭch'yŏ chushigessŏyo?

Toksu Palace?

**Student :** Certainly, yes. Go down this way (*pointing*) to the first traffic light and then turn left. The main gate of the palace is on your left. You can't miss it.

**Miss Wilson :** That's very clear.
Thanks a lot.

**Student :** Not at all.

3. In Front of the City Hall

**A Motorist :** I am trying to get to Insa-dong, please.

**Policeman :** Follow this big road till you get to the National Museum.Turn right and go over a little hill. Bear to the right at the next intersection.

**A Motorist :** Is it far from here?

덕수궁 가는 길을 가르쳐 주시겠어요?

S : Ne, ch'ŏtchae shinhodŭngkkaji i kirŭl naeryŏgashidaga oentchogŭro toragaseyo. Oentchoge (tŏksugungŭi) taemuni issŭmnida.
네, 첫째 신호등까지 이 길을 (가리키면서) 내려가시다가 왼쪽으로 돌아가세요. 왼쪽에 (덕수궁의) 대문이 있습니다.

W : Chal arassŭmnida.
Taedanhi kamsahamnida.
잘 알았습니다.
대단히 감사합니다.

S : Ch'ŏnmaneyo.
천만에요.

## 3. 시청 앞에서

M : Insadong-e karyŏnŭndeyo.
인사동에 가려는데요.

P : Kungnip pangmulgwani naol ttaekkaji i kirŭl ttara kashipshio.
Orŭnp'yŏnŭro torasŏ chagŭn ŏndŏgŭl nŏmŏgashipshio.
Taŭm kyoch'arokkaji pisŭdŭmhi orŭntchogŭro toseyo.
국립 박물관이 나올 때까지 이 길을 따라 가십시오. 오른편으로 돌아서 작은 언덕을 넘어가십시오. 다음 교차로까지 비스듬히 오른쪽으로 도세요.

M : Yŏgisŏ mŏmnikka? 여기서 멉니까?

**Policeman :** No, it's near. It's only a five minute drive.

**A Motorist :** You are very kind.

**Policeman :** Not at all, sir.

4. At the Youi-do Apartment Complex

**Mrs. Mintz :** Excuse me. Could you tell me which is the No. 8 apartment building?

**Florist :** Is it Samhwa Apartment or Hanyang Apartment?

**Mrs. Mintz :** Oh, I believe it's Samhwa Apartment.

**Florist :** Then, go around that fountain to your right. Turn left at the corner drugstore. The No. 8 building is the second one on your right.

**Mrs. Mintz :** Thank you. I think I'll buy some of these pink roses for my hostess.

**P** : Anio, kakkapsŭmnida. Ch'aro obun kŏllimnida.
아니오, 가깝습니다. 차로 오분 걸립니다.

**M** : Kamsahamnida.
감사합니다.

**P** : Ch'ŏnmanŭi malssŭmimnida.
천만의 말씀입니다.

## 4. 여의도 아파트에서

**M** : Shillyehamnida. Ŏnŭ kŏshi p'altong kŏnmurinji karŭch'yŏ chushigessŭmnikka?
실례합니다. 어느 것이 팔동 건물인지 가르쳐 주시겠습니까?

**F** : Samhwa ap'at'ŭimnikka, Hanyang ap'at'ŭ marimnikka?
삼화 아파트입니까, 한양 아파트 말입니까?

**M** : Ama, Samhwa ap'at'ŭil kŏmnida.
아마, 삼화 아파트일 겁니다.

**F** : Kŭrŏmyŏn orŭntchogŭro chŏ punsurŭl ttara kaseyo. Mot'ungi yakkugesŏ oentchogŭro toragaseyo. P'altongŭn orŭnp'yŏnesŏ tultchaepŏnimnida.
그러면 오른쪽으로 저 분수를 따라 가세요. 모퉁이 약국에서 왼쪽으로 돌아가세요. 팔동은 오른편에서 둘째 번입니다.

**M** : Kamsahamnida. Chipchuinege punhong changmikkoch'ŭl chom sada tŭrinŭn ke chok'etkunyo.
감사합니다. 집주인에게 분홍 장미꽃을 좀 사다 드리는 게 좋겠군요.

**Florist :** Thank you.

## 5. Ginseng Tea

(*Mr. Deans is talking with his friend Mr. Kim.*)

**Mr. Deans :** I've heard that Korean ginseng tea is good for the health. Where is a good place to buy it?

**Mr. Kim :** You can find it almost anywhere, but the best place is at the Ulchi-ro intersection.

**Mr. Deans :** Oh, is that so? Which side of the intersection exactly?

**Mr. Kim :** Both on the east and the north sides.

Just walk around the intersection and you will find a number of shops which sell all kinds of ginseng products.

F : Kamsahamnida.
감사합니다.

## 5. 인 삼 차

(Mr. 딘즈와 Mr. 김과의 대화)

D : Han-guk insamch'aga kŏn-gange chot'ago tŭrŏssŭmnida.
Kŭgŏl saryŏmyŏn ŏdi kamyŏn choŭlkkayo?
한국 인삼차가 건강에 좋다고 들었습니다. 그걸 사려면 어디 가면 좋을까요?

K : Ŏdiesŏna kuhal su issŭmnidaman, kajang choŭn kosŭn Ŭlchiro negŏrie issŭmnida.
어디에서나 구할 수 있습니다만, 가장 좋은 곳은 을지로 네거리에 있습니다.

D : Ăh, kŭraeyo.
Chŏnghwak'i kŭ negŏri ŏnŭ tchogimnikka?
아, 그래요.
정확히 그 네거리 어느 쪽입니까?

K : Tongtchokkwa puktchoge ta issŭmnida.
Negŏrirŭl ttara kŏrŏ toraganoramyŏn yŏrŏ kaji insam chep'umŭl p'anŭn sangjŏmi mani issŭmnida.
동쪽과 북쪽에 다 있습니다. 네거리를 따라 걸어 돌아가노라면 여러 가지 인삼 제품을 파는 상점이 많이 있습니다.

**Mr. Deans :** Can you come along with me if you are not busy?

**Mr. Kim :** Yes, certainly. (*With pleasure*)

## 6. Korean Chests

**Miss Church :** I want to buy some Korean chests. Where do you suggest that I go?

**Miss Chung :** Do you want antiques or modern pieces?

**Miss Church :** Antiques if they are not too expensive.

**Miss Chung :** You may be able to find what you want in Insa-dong. It's a famous street where all kinds of Korean art works are sold.

**Miss Church :** That's interesting.
Now, how do I get there?

**Miss Chung :** Do you remember Pagoda Park?

**D** : Pappŭshiji anŭshimyŏn chŏwa kach'i kajushige-ssŭmnikka?
바쁘시지 않으시면 저와 같이 가주시겠습니까?

**K** : Ne, kŭrŏk'e hajyo. 네, 그렇게 하죠.

## 6. 한국의 장

**Ch:** Han-gugŭi changŭl chom sago ship'ŭndeyo. Ŏdiesŏ kuhanŭn ke chok'essŭmnikka?
한국의 장을 좀 사고 싶은데요.
어디에서 구하는 게 좋겠습니까?

**Cg:** Koltongp'umŭl wŏnhashinŭnji, hogŭn hyŏndaeŭi kŏsŭl wŏnhashinŭnjiyo?
골동품을 원하시는지, 혹은 현대의 것을 원하시는지요?

**Ch:** Nŏmu pissaji anŭmyŏn koltongp'umŭl sago ship-sŭmnida.
너무 비싸지 않으면 골동품을 사고 싶습니다.

**Cg:** Insadonge kashimyŏn maŭme tŭshinŭn kŏsŭl ch'a-jŭl su issŭl kŏshimnida. Kŭ kosŭn yŏrŏ kajiŭi Han-guk misulp'umŭl p'anŭn kosŭro irŭmnan kŏ-riimnida.
인사동에 가시면 마음에 드시는 것을 찾을 수 있을 것입니다. 그 곳은 여러 가지의 한국 미술품을 파는 곳으로 이름난 거리입니다.

**Ch:** Kŭgŏt ch'am hŭngmiropkunyo. Kŭrŏm ŏttŏk'e kal su innayo?
그것 참 흥미롭군요. 그럼 어떻게 갈 수 있나요?

**Cg:** P'agoda kongwŏn saenggangnashijyo?
파고다 공원 생각나시죠?

**Miss Church :** Yes.

**Miss Chung :** That's the street west of the park to Anguk-dong.

**Miss Church :** Thank you.

**Miss Chung :** Not at all.

Special Product of Korea, Ginseng

**Ch:** Ne.
네.

**Cg:** Kŭ kongwŏn sŏtchogesŏ Anguktongŭro kanŭn kirimnida.
그 공원 서쪽에서 안국동으로 가는 길입니다.

**Ch:** Kamsahamnida. 감사합니다.

**Cg:** Ch'ŏnmaneyo. 천만에요.

Korean Chest

# III. TRANSPORTATIONS

## □ Useful Expressions

1. Please show me your passport.
2. Please fill in this card.
3. Shall I weigh your baggage?
4. I want this bag checked.
5. Thank you for coming out to see me off.
6. I'm going to visit Kyongju next week.
7. Are you traveling by bus?
8. The plane will leave on time.
9. It will take about seven hours.
   It will take about two and a half hours to get there.
10. Will you draw me a simple map?

# Ⅲ. 여행(수송)

## □ 많이 쓰는 표현

1. Yŏkwŏnŭl chom poyŏ chushipshio.
   여권을 좀 보여 주십시오.
2. I k'adŭe chŏgŭshipshio.
   이 카드에 적으십시오.
3. Tangshinŭi chimŭl tara polkkayo?
   당신의 짐을 달아 볼까요?
4. I kabangŭl pwa chushipshio.
   이 가방을 봐 주십시오.
5. Chŏnsong nawa chusyŏsŏ kamsahamnida.
   전송 나와 주셔서 감사합니다.
6. Taŭmchue Kyŏngjurŭl pangmunharyŏmnida.
   다음주에 경주를 방문하렵니다.
7. Pŏsŭro yŏhaenghashiryŏmnikka?
   버스로 여행하시렵니까?
8. Pihaenggiga che shigane ttŏnamnida.
   비행기가 제 시간에 떠납니다.
9. Yak ilgop shigan kŏllil kŏshimnida. Kŏgie toch'ak'aryŏmyŏn yak tu shigan pani kŏllil kŏshimnida.
   약 일곱 시간 걸릴 것입니다. 거기에 도착하려면 약 두 시간 반이 걸릴 것입니다.
10. Kandanhan chidorŭl kŭryŏ chushigessŭmnikka?
    간단한 지도를 그려 주시겠습니까?

11. Where's the dining car?

12. What is the name of this town?

13. Where do I get permission to visit Panmunjom?

14. I'd like a night tour of Seoul.

15. I am going to stay in Kyongju about a week.

16. What number bus goes to the station?

17. Does this bus go to Yongsan?

18. How long does it take to get there?

19. Take me to the National Museum.

20. How much do I owe you?

21. How much is the fare?

22. Are the runs frequent?

23. Are there a lot of buses?

24. What time do we get to Taejon?

11. Shiktangch'anŭn ŏdie issŭmnikka?
식당차는 어디에 있습니까?
12. I toshiŭi irŭmŭn muŏshimnikka?
이 도시의 이름은 무엇입니까?
13. P'anmunjŏmŭl pangmunharyŏmyŏn ŏdiesŏ hŏgarŭl passŭmnikka?
판문점을 방문하려면 어디에서 허가를 받습니까?
14. Sŏurŭi yagan kwan-gwangŭl hago shipsŭmnida.
서울의 야간 관광을 하고 싶습니다.
15. Han chuil tongan Kyŏngjue mŏmullyŏgo hamnida. 한 주일 동안 경주에 머물려고 합니다.
16. Myŏt pŏn pŏsŭga yŏge kamnikka?
몇 번 버스가 역에 갑니까?
17. I pŏsŭga Yongsane kamnikka?
이 버스가 용산에 갑니까?
18. Kŏgikkaji ŏlmana kŏllimnikka?
거기까지 얼마나 걸립니까?
19. Kungnip pangmulgwankkaji teryŏda chuseyo.
국립 박물관까지 데려다 주세요.
20. Ŏlmaimnikka?
얼마입니까?
21. Yogŭmŭn ŏlmaimnikka? 요금은 얼마입니까?
22. Ch'ap'yŏni chaju issŭmnikka?
차편이 자주 있습니까?
23. Pŏsŭga mani issŭmnikka?
버스가 많이 있습니까?
24. Myŏt shie Taejŏne toch'ak'amnikka?
몇 시에 대전에 도착합니까?

25. We'll get there by six.

26. I want two first class ticket to Pusan, please.

27. I would like a ticket from Pusan to Cheju.

28. Please give me a round trip ticket to Kwangju.

29. I'd like to make a reservation for a flight to Jeju on April 15th.

30. I want to reserve a room at the Chosun Hotel.

## 1. Bus

**Mr. Bruce :** Excuse me. What number bus goes to Changchung Gymnasium?

**A Young Lady :** There are many, but bus No.75 is least crowded at this hour of the day.

25. Yŏsŏssikkajinŭn toch'ak'al kŏshimnida.
여섯시까지는 도착할 것입니다.
26. Pusankkaji iltŭngp'yo tu chang chushipshio.
부산까지 일등표 두 장 주십시오.
27. Pusanesŏ Chejukkaji p'yo han chang chushipshio.
부산에서 제주까지 표 한 장 주십시오.
28. Kwangjukkaji wangbokp'yo han chang chushipshio.
광주까지 왕복표 한 장 주십시오.
29. Sawŏl shiboil Cheju kanŭn pihaenggip'yo han chang yeyak'aryŏgo hamnida.
사월 십오일 제주 가는 비행기표 한 장 예약하려고 합니다.
30. Chosŏn hot'ere pang hana yeyak'ago shipsŭmnida.
조선 호텔에 방 하나 예약하고 싶습니다.

## 1. 버 스

**B** : Malssŭm chom murŭlkkayo?
Myŏt pŏn pŏsŭga Changch'ung ch'eyukkwane kamnikka?
말씀 좀 물을까요?
몇 번 버스가 장충 체육관에 갑니까?

**L** : Mani issŭmnidaman i shigane kajang pumbiji annŭn kŏsŭn ch'ilshibobŏn pŏsŭimnida.
많이 있습니다만, 이 시간에 가장 붐비지 않는 것은 칠십오번 버스입니다.

**Mr. Bruce :** Thank you.

**A Young Lady :** Oh, here comes No.154 that also goes to Changchung Gymnasium.

It's nearly empty.

Why don't you get on this one?

**Mr. Bruce :** Thank you. You are very kind.

## 2. In Pusan

**Mr. McCuine :** Does this bus go to Haeundae?

**Guide :** Yes, but via Tongnae. Take bus No.5 to get there a little quicker.

**Mr. McCuine :** Thank you. But, how long does this bus take to get there?

**Guide :** About an hour and a quarter.

**Mr. McCuine :** And bus No.5?

**Guide :** Less than an hour, sir.

B : Kamsahamnida.
감사합니다.

L : Ah, yŏgi paegoshipsabŏn pŏsŭga onŭn-gunyo. I gŏtto Changch'ung ch'eyukkwanŭro kamnida. Kŏŭi piŏ itkunyo. Igŏsŭl t'ashijiyo.
아, 여기 백오십사번 버스가 오는군요. 이것도 장충 체육관으로 갑니다. 거의 비어 있군요. 이것을 타시지요.

B : Chŏngmal komapsŭmnida.
정말 고맙습니다.

## 2. 부산에서

M : I pŏsŭga Haeundaero kamnikka?
이 버스가 해운대로 갑니까?

G : Ne, kŭrŏnde Tongnaerŭl kŏch'yŏsŏ kamnida. Obŏn pŏsŭrŭl t'ashimyŏn chom ppalli kashil su issŭmnida.
네, 그런데 동래를 거쳐서 갑니다. 오번 버스를 타시면 좀 빨리 가실 수 있습니다.

M : Kamsahamnida. Kŭrŏnde i pŏsŭro kamyŏn ŏlmana kŏllimnikka?
감사합니다. 그런데 이 버스로 가면 얼마나 걸립니까?

G : Han shigan shibobuntchŭmiyo.
한 시간 십오분쯤이요.

M : Kŭrŏm obŏn pŏsŭnŭnyo?
그럼 오번 버스는요?

G : Han shigan inaeimnida.
한 시간 이내입니다.

**Mr. McCuine :** Well, I'm not in a hurry. And I've never seen Tongnae. I'd better try this one.

**Guide :** If you please. Watch your step!

**Mr. McCuine :** Thank you.

## 3. Getting around in Taxi

**Mr. Johnson :** Taxi! Taxi!

**Taxi Driver :** Please get in.

**Mr. Johnson :** Take me to the International Post Office, please.

Taxi Driver : Yes, sir. You mean the one at the Mok-dong apartment complex.

**Mr. Johnson :** That's right. I want to pick up a package.

How long will it take to get there?

**Taxi Driver :** It'll take about 15 minutes, sir.

**M** : Kŭraeyo. Nanŭn kŭp'aji anssŭmnida.
Kŭrigo Tongnaerŭl ajik mot poassŭmnida. I pŏsŭrŭl t'anŭn kŏshi chok'etkunyo.
그래요. 나는 급하지 않습니다.
그리고 동래를 아직 못 보았습니다. 이 버스를 타는 것이 좋겠군요.

**G** : Kŭrŏshijyo. Kyedan choshimhaseyo.
그러시죠. 계단 조심하세요.

**M** : Kamsahamnida.
감사합니다.

## 3. 택시를 탈 때

**J** : T'aekshi, t'aekshi.
택시, 택시.

**D** : Ŏsŏ t'ashipshio.
어서 타십시오.

**J** : Kukche uch'egukkaji kapshida.
국제 우체국까지 갑시다.

**D** : Ne, Mok-dong ap'at'ŭ tanjie innŭn kŏt marimnikka?
네, 목동 아파트 단지에 있는 것 말입니까?

**J** : Kŭraeyo.
Sop'o hanarŭl ch'ajŭryŏ hamnida.
Kŏgikkaji ŏlmana kŏllimnikka?
그래요. 소포 하나를 찾으려 합니다.
거기까지 얼마나 걸립니까?

**D** : Yak shibobun kŏllimnida.
약 십오분 걸립니다.

**Mr. Johnson :** I'm not in a hurry. Please drive carefully.

**Taxi Driver :** All right, sir.

**Taxi Driver :** Here we are, sir.

**Mr. Johnson :** How much do I owe you?

**Taxi Driver :** That's 3,500 won, sir.

**Mr. Johnson :** Here you are. Thank you.

**Taxi Driver :** Thank you. Good-bye.

## 4. Subway

**Mr. Swift :** I want to visit a friend of mine near Chongnyangni. What is the best way to get there?

**Mr. Yang :** The subway is the best. It is comfortable and fast.

**Mr. Swift :** Oh, yes. How long will it take to get there?

**Mr. Yang :** About 15 minutes.

J : Kŭp'aji anayo. Choshimhaesŏ kapshida.
급하지 않아요. 조심해서 갑시다.

D : Ne, kŭrŏk'e hajyo.
네, 그렇게 하죠.

D : Ta wassŭmnida.
다 왔습니다.

J : Ŏlmaimnikka?
얼마입니까?

D : Samch'ŏnobaegwŏnimnida.
삼천오백원입니다.

J : Yŏgi issŭmnida. Kamsahamnida.
여기 있습니다. 감사합니다.

D : Annyŏnghi kashipshio.
안녕히 가십시오.

## 4. 지 하 철

S : Ch'ŏngnyangni kŭnch'ŏe innŭn nae ch'in-gurŭl pangmunhago ship'ŭndeyo. Kŏgie karyŏmyŏn muŏsŭl t'anŭn kŏshi kajang choŭlkkayo?
청량리 근처에 있는 내 친구를 방문하고 싶은데요. 거기에 가려면 무엇을 타는 것이 가장 좋을까요?

Y : Chihach'ŏri cheil chok'essŭmnida. Aju p'yŏnanhago pparŭmnida.
지하철이 제일 좋겠습니다. 아주 편안하고 빠릅니다.

S : Ne, ŏlmana kŏllilkkayo?
네, 얼마나 걸릴까요?

Y : Yak shibobun kŏllimnida. 약 십오분 걸립니다.

**Mr. Swift :** That's fast enough. And how much is the fare?

**Mr. Yang :** The basic fare is 500 won. It depends on the distance.

**Mr. Swift :** That's good. Are the runs frequent?

**Mr. Yang :** Certainly. Every three minutes, I think.

**Mr. Swift :** That seems quite convenient.

## 5. Express Bus

**Mr. Yu :** Does this bus go to Kangnung?

**Conductor :** Yes. Your ticket, please.

**Mr. Yu :** Here you are, two.

**Conductor :** Thank you. Watch your step!

S : Kŭmanhamyŏn pparŭgunyo.
Yogŭmŭn olmajyo?
그만하면 빠르군요.
요금은 얼마죠?

Y : Kibonyongŭmŭn obaegwŏnimnida.
Kŏliettala talayo.
기본요금은 500원입니다.
거리에 따라 달라요.

S : Kŭgŏt chok'unyo. Ch'ap'yŏni chaju issŭmnikka?
그것 좋군요. 차편이 자주 있습니까?

Y : Kŭrŏmyo.
Ama sambunmada issŭl kŏyeyo.
그럼요.
아마 삼분마다 있을 거예요.

S : Kŭgŏt chŏngmal p'yŏllihagunyo.
그것 정말 편리하군요.

## 5. 고속 버스

Y : I pŏsŭga Kangnŭng kanayo?
이 버스가 강릉 가나요?

C : Ne, p'yo chom popshida.
네, 표 좀 봅시다.

Y : Yŏgi tu changiyo.
여기 두 장이요.

C : Kamsahamnida. Kyedan choshimhaseyo.
감사합니다.
계단 조심하세요.

**Mr. Yu :** Here we are. Our seats are No. 15 & No. 16.

Would you like to take the window side?

**Mr. Williams :** It doesn't matter. All right, I'll sit there.

*(They settle down in their seats.)*

**Mr. Williams :** What time do we get to Kangnung, Mr. Yu?

**Mr. Yu :** It takes about four hours if the traffic is not too heavy. So we'll get there by five.

It used to take more than eight hours before the express way was built.

**Mr. Williams :** That's great progress. The weather is really excellent today. I am really looking forward to the views of the mountains you talked about.

Y : Yŏgigunyo. Uri charinŭn shibobŏn, shimyukpŏnijyo.
Ch'angka-e anjŭshigessŏyo?
여기군요. 우리 자리는 십오번, 십육번이죠.
창가에 앉으시겠어요?

W : Sanggwanŏpsŏyo.
Ne, chega kŏgi antchyo.
상관없어요.
네, 제가 거기 앉죠.

(그들은 자리를 잡았다.)

W : Yu sŏnsaengnim, myŏt shie Kangnŭnge toch'ak'alkkayo?
유 선생님, 몇 시에 강릉에 도착할까요?

Y : Kyot'ongi kwahi pumbiji anŭmyŏn ne shigan kŏllimnida. Kŭrŏnikka tasŏssikkajinŭn toch'aktoel kŏmnida. Kosok toroga saenggigi chŏnenŭn yŏdŏl shigan isangina kŏllyŏtchiyo.
교통이 과히 붐비지 않으면 네 시간 걸립니다. 그러니까 다섯시까지는 도착될 겁니다. 고속 도로가 생기기 전에는 여덟 시간 이상이나 걸렸지요.

W : Koengjanghan palchŏnigunyo. Onŭl kihunŭn chŏngmal kŭmanimnida. Nanŭn chŏngmal Yu sŏnsaengnimi malssŭmhashin san-gyŏngch'iga ŏttŏlchi kidaedoenŭn-gunyo.
굉장한 발전이군요. 오늘 기후는 정말로 그만입니다. 나는 정말 유 선생님이 말씀하신 산경치가 어떨지 기대되는군요.

**Mr. Yu** : You won't be disappointed.

## 6. Train

(*At the ticket office*)

**Miss Jackson** : I want a ticket to Ch'unch'ŏn, please.

**Clerk** : 4,200 won, please.

**Miss Jackson** : Here it is. What time does the next train leave?

**Clerk** : At 11, Miss.
There's one every hour on the hour.

**Miss Jackson** : And how long does it take to get there?

**Clerk** : It takes just two hours.

**Miss Jackson** : Thank you. Good-bye.

**Clerk** : Good-bye. Have a nice trip.

Y : Ama kidaee ŏgŭnnaji anŭl kŏmnida.
아마 기대에 어긋나지 않을 겁니다.

## 6. 기 차

(출찰구에서)

J : Ch'unchŏn kanŭn p'yo hana chuseyo.
춘천 가는 표 하나 주세요.

C : Sach'ŏnibaegwŏnimnida.
사천이백원입니다.

J : Yŏgi issŏyo. Taŭm kich'anŭn myŏt shie ttŏnamnikka?
여기 있어요. 다음 기차는 몇 시에 떠납니까?

C : Yŏrhanshie issŏyo. Shiganmada chŏngshie issŭmnida.
열한시에 있어요. 시간마다 정시에 있습니다.

J : Kŏgie toch'ak'aryŏmyŏn ŏlmana kŏllimnikka?
거기에 도착하려면 얼마나 걸립니까?

J : Kkok tu shigan kŏllimnida.
꼭 두 시간 걸립니다.

J : Kamsahamnida. Annyŏnghi kyeshipshio.
감사합니다. 안녕히 계십시오.

C : Annyŏnghi kaseyo. Chŭlgŏun yŏhaeng hashigi paramnida.
안녕히 가세요. 즐거운 여행 하시기 바랍니다.

## 7. At the Airlines Office

**Clerk :** Good afternoon. May I help you?

**Mr. White :** Yes, I would like to buy tickets from Pusan to Cheju and back to Seoul.

**Clerk :** When would you like to leave Pusan for Cheju, sir?

**Mr. White :** I'd like to go on Tuesday May 6th in the afternoon. I want to stay on Cheju-do, for about three days, and then return to Seoul on the 9th.

**Clerk :** All right, sir. Flight 35 leaves Pusan at 4:30 in the afternoon and arrives at Cheju at 5:20.

**Mr. White :** That seems fine to me. I'll have enough time to wash up (to rest a while) before dinner.

## 7. 항공 여행사에서

C : Annyŏnghaseyo. Towa tŭrilkkayo?
안녕하세요. 도와 드릴까요?

W : Ne, Pusanesŏ Chejukkaji, kŭrigo Sŏullo toraonŭn p'yorŭl sago ship'ŭndeyo.
네, 부산에서 제주까지, 그리고 서울로 돌아오는 표를 사고 싶은데요.

C : Ŏnje Pusansŏ Chejuro ttŏnashiryŏmnikka, sŏnsaengnim?
언제 부산서 제주로 떠나시렵니까, 선생님?

W : Owŏl yugil hwayoil ohue ttŏnaryŏgo hamnida. Chejudo-e samilgan mŏmulgo kuire Sŏure toraogo shipsŭmnida.
오월 육일 화요일 오후에 떠나려고 합니다.
제주도에 삼일간 머물고 구일에 서울에 돌아오고 싶습니다.

C : Arassŭmnida. Pihaeng samshibop'yŏni ohu neshi samshippune Pusanŭl ttŏna Chejue tasŏssi ishippune toch'ak'amnida.
알았습니다. 비행 삼십오편이 오후 네시 삼십분에 부산을 떠나 제주에 다섯시 이십분에 도착합니다.

W : Chegenŭn kŭgŏshi chok'essŭmnida. Chŏnyŏk mŏkki chŏne sesuhal(chogŭm shwil) shigani nŏngnŏk'agetkunyo.
제게는 그것이 좋겠습니다.
저녁 먹기 전에 세수할(조금 쉴) 시간이 넉넉하겠군요.

**Clerk** : Then on the 9th you'll be able to get back to Seoul by Korean Air Flight 203 leaving Cheju at 5:00 and arriving in Seoul at 5:50.

**Mr. White** : That's really fast. Well I'd like to reserve two seats for these flights. How much will that come to?

**Clerk** : Just a second, please.
That'll be 151,600 won, sir.

**Mr. White** : Here you are.

**Clerk** : Thank you. Your flights are all reserved now, sir. Would you like us to reserve your hotel, too?

**Mr. White** : No, thank you. We'll be staying at my friends.

**Clerk** : All right, sir. Have a nice trip.

**Mr. White** : Thank you.

**Clerk** : Good-bye, Sir.

**Mr. White** : Good-bye.

C : Kŭrigo kuil tasŏssie Chejurŭl ttŏna tasŏssi oship-pune Sŏure toch'ak'anŭn Taehan Hanggong igongsam p'yŏnŭro toraoshil su issŭmnida.
그리고 구일 다섯시에 제주를 떠나 다섯시 오십분에 서울에 도착하는 대한항공 이공삼 편으로 돌아오실 수 있습니다.

W : Kŭgŏt chŏngmal pparŭgunyo. Kŭrŏt'amyŏn kŭ pi-haenggie tu charirŭl yeyak'agessŭmnida. Yogŭmi-ŏlmana toemnikka?
그것 정말 빠르군요. 그렇다면 그 비행기에 두 자리를 예약하겠습니다. 요금이 얼마나 됩니까?

C : Chamkkanman kidariseyo. **Shibomanch'ŏnyuk-paegwŏni** toegessŭmnida.
잠깐만 기다리세요. 십오만천육백원이 되겠습니다.

W : Yŏgi issŭmnida.
여기 있습니다.

C : Kamsahamnida. Ije yeyagi ta toeŏssŭmnida. Ho-t'el yeyakto hae tŭrilkkayo?
감사합니다. 이제 예약이 다 되었습니다. 호텔 예약도 해 드릴까요?

W : Anio. Ch'in-gu chibe mŏmulge toel kŏshimnida.
아니오. 친구 집에 머물게 될 것입니다.

C : Kŭrŏseyo. Chŭlgŏun yŏhaengŭl hashigi paramni-da.
그러세요. 즐거운 여행을 하시기 바랍니다.

W : Kamsahamnida. 감사합니다.

C : Annyŏnghi kashipshio. 안녕히 가십시오.

W : Annyŏnghi kyeshipshio. 안녕히 계십시오.

# IV. RESTAURANTS

## □ Useful Expressions

1. Where is the famous Korean restaurant near here?
2. Are there any good Korean restaurants near here?
3. Where can I find some western food in this town?
4. A table for four, please.
5. This table is reserved.
6. This is a very comfortable place.
7. Menu, please.
8. What would you like?
9. What would you like to drink?
10. What is the speciality of this restaurant?

# IV. 레스토랑

## □ 많이 쓰는 표현

1. I kŭnch'ŏe yumyŏnghan Han-guk shiktangi ŏdi issŭmnikka?
   이 근처에 유명한 한국 식당이 어디 있습니까?
2. I kŭnch'ŏe choŭn Han-guk ŭmshikchŏmi issŭmnikka?
   이 근처에 좋은 한국 음식점이 있습니까?
3. I shinaee yangshikchibi issŭmnikka?
   이 시내에 양식집이 있습니까?
4. Ne saram chari put'ak'amnida.
   네 사람 자리 부탁합니다.
5. I charinŭn yeyaktoeŏ issŭmnida.
   이 자리는 예약되어 있습니다.
6. Yŏginŭn aju p'yŏnanhan koshimnida.
   여기는 아주 편안한 곳입니다.
7. Menyu chom chuseyo.
   메뉴 좀 주세요.
8. Muŏsŭl tŭshilkkayo?
   무엇을 드실까요?
9. Muŏsŭl mashigessŭmnikka?
   무엇을 마시겠습니까?
10. I kosesŏ charhanŭn ŭmshigi muŏshimnikka?
    이 곳에서 잘하는 음식이 무엇입니까?

11. One more beer, please.

12. How is it cooked?

13. Is it very (pepper) hot?

14. Will you have some?

15. Two more portions of *pulgogi*, please.

16. Have you tried *shinsollo?*

17. I'd like to try that.

## 1. At the Hotel Restaurant

*(Mr. Wide and Mr. Ko enter the hotel restaurant.)*

**Waiter :** Good afternoon, sir.

**Mr. Ko :** We'd like a table on the window side.

**Waiter :** All right, sir. This way, please.

*(They sit down at the table.)*

**Waiter :** Here's the menu. The Korean dishes

11. Maekchu hana tŏ chushipshio.
맥주 하나 더 주십시오.
12. Ŏttŏk'e yorihaennayo?
어떻게 요리했나요?
13. Aju maepsŭmnikka?
아주 맵습니까?
14. Chom tŏ tŭshigessŏyo?
좀 더 드시겠어요?
15. Pulgogi iinbun tŏ chushijiyo.
불고기 이인분 더 주시지요.
16. Shinsŏllo tŭshin chŏgi issŏyo?
신선로 드신 적이 있어요?
17. Kŭgŏt matpogo shipsŭmnida.
그것 맛보고 싶습니다.

## 1. 호텔 레스토랑에서

(Mr. 와이드와 Mr. 고는 호텔 레스토랑에 들어간다.)

**W** : Annyŏnghashimnikka?
안녕하십니까?

**K** : Ch'angkaŭi t'eibŭre anjassŭmyŏn chok'essŭmnida.
창가의 테이블에 앉았으면 좋겠습니다.

**W** : Arassŭmnida. Iriro oshipshio.
알았습니다. 이리로 오십시오.

(그들은 자리에 앉는다.)

**W** : Yŏgi menyu issŭmnida. Han-guk ŭmshigŭn orŭnp'yŏne chŏk'yŏ issŭmnida.
여기 메뉴 있습니다. 한국 음식은 오른편에 적혀 있습니다.

are listed on the right side.

**Mr. Ko :** I see. Mr. Wide, what would you like to have?

**Mr. Wide :** Well, I'd rather go for a Korean dinner today.

I like a variety of small side dishes.

How about you, Mr. Ko?

**Mr. Ko :** I think I want a western dish.

(*To the waiter*) What's today's special?

**Waiter :** Fried shrimp, sir. They are really good today.

**Mr. Ko :** All right. One Korean dinner and one special.

**Waiter :** Yes, sir. And what would you like to drink?

**Mr. Wide :** I'd like just a small beer.

**Mr. Ko :** So would I. (*To the waiter*) Two

**K** : Algessŭmnida. Waidŭ ssi. Muŏsŭl tŭshigessŏyo?
알겠습니다. 와이드 씨, 무엇을 드시겠어요?

**Wi**: Kŭlsseyo. Nanŭn onŭrŭn Han-gukshik chŏnyŏgŭl tŭlgessŏyo.

Nanŭn yŏrŏ kaji panch'anŭl choahaeyo. Ko sŏnsaengnimŭn muŏsŭl tŭshigessŏyo?
글쎄요. 나는 오늘은 한국식 저녁을 들겠어요.
나는 여러 가지 반찬을 좋아해요.
고 선생님은 무엇을 드시겠어요?

**K** : Chŏnŭn yangshigŭl hagessŏyo. Onŭl t'ukshigŭn muŏshimnikka?
저는 양식을 하겠어요. (웨이터에게) 오늘 특식은 무엇입니까?

**W** : Saeu t'wigimimnida.

Onŭrŭn saeuga ch'am chossŭmnida.
새우 튀김입니다.
오늘은 새우가 참 좋습니다.

**K** : Kŭrŏm, hanjŏngshik hanawa t'ukshik hana chuseyo.
그럼, 한정식 하나와 특식 하나 주세요.

**W** : Ne, mashil kŏsŭn muŏsŭro hashilkkayo?
네, 마실 것은 무엇으로 하실까요?

**Wi**: Chŏnŭn maekchu chagŭn kŏt hanaman hagessŏyo.
저는 맥주 작은 것 하나만 하겠어요.

**K** : Chŏdo kŭrŏgessŏyo. Maekchu chagŭn pyŏng tul chuseyo.

저도 그러겠어요. (웨이터에게) 맥주 작은 병 둘 주세요.

small beers, please.

**Waiter** : All right, sir.

## 2. At a Korean Restaurant

**Mr. Shim** : We had a pleasant walk today, didn't we?

**Mr. Walker** : Yes, that was really wonderful. Let's have a good dinner some place.

**Mr. Shim** : Fine. Shall we have *pulgogi?*

**Mr. Walker** : That's a good idea. Oh, I see a restaurant over there.

**Mr. Shim** : Yes, that's a famous one. Let's cross the street here.

* * *

**Waiter** : Good evening (Welcome), sir.

**Mr. Shim** : A table for two in a quiet corner, please.

**Waiter** : Yes, sir. This way, please.

W : Ne, arassŭmnida.
네, 알았습니다.

## 2. 한국 음식점에서

S : Onŭl ch'am yuk'waehan sanch'aegŭl haessŏyo. Kŭrŏch'yo?
오늘 참 유쾌한 산책을 했어요. 그렇죠?

W : Ne, chŏngmal choassŏyo. Ŏdi kasŏ madinnŭn chŏnyŏgŭl hapshida.
네, 정말 좋았어요. 어디 가서 맛있는 저녁을 합시다.

S : Pulgogirŭl halkkayo?
불고기를 할까요?

W : Choŭn saenggagimnida. Ah, chŏgi shiktangi hana itkunyo.
좋은 생각입니다. 아, 저기 식당이 하나 있군요.

S : Ne, cho kosŭn yumyŏnghan koshimnida.
Yŏgisŏ kirŭl kŏnnŏgapshida.
네, 저 곳은 유명한 곳입니다.
여기서 길을 건너갑시다.

*   *   *

W : Annyŏnghashimnikka, ŏsŏ oshipshio.
안녕하십니까, 어서 오십시오.

S : Choyonghan kose tu saram chari put'ak'amnida.
조용한 곳에 두 사람 자리 부탁합니다.

W : Ne, iriro oshipshio.
네, 이리로 오십시오.

(*At the table*)

**Waiter :** (*Hands each a moist towel*)
What would you like to have?

**Mr. Shim :** First to begin with, bring us two portions of *pulgogi*, please.

**Waiter :** Yes, sir. Shall I bring rice now?

**Mr. Shim :** No, not now. Mr. Walker, would you rather have *naengmyon* after the *pulgogi?*

**Mr. Walker :** Yes, I've tried that combination, and I like that particular taste.

**Mr. Shim :** And how about *soju* with the *pulgogi*?

That's typically Korean.

**Mr. Walker :** Well, it's perfectly all right with me.

You know I am quickly becoming Koreanized.

(식탁에서)

W : (물수건을 각 사람에게 넘기며)
Muŏsŭl tŭshilkkayo?
무엇을 드실까요?

S : Mŏnjŏ pulgogi iinbunbut'ŏ kajyŏoseyo.
먼저 불고기 이인분부터 가져오세요.

W : Ne, pabŭl chigŭm kajyŏolkkayo?
네, 밥을 지금 가져올까요?

S : Anio, chigŭm malgoyo.
Wŏk'ŏ ssi, pulgogirŭl tŭshin hue naengmyŏnŭro hashigessŭmnikka?
아니오, 지금 말고요.
워커 씨, 불고기를 드신 후에 냉면으로 하시겠습니까?

W1: Ne, chŏdo kŭrŏk'e mŏgŏ poassŭmnida.
Kŭrigo kŭ tokt'ŭk'an mashi chossŭmnida.
네, 저도 그렇게 먹어 보았습니다. 그리고 그 독특한 맛이 좋습니다.

S : Pulgogiwa kach'i sojunŭn ŏttŏseyo?
Igŏn chŏnhyŏngjŏgin Han-gukshigimnida.
불고기와 같이 소주는 어떠세요?
이건 전형적인 한국식입니다.

W1: Chŏ, chŏnŭn chŏngmal kwaench'anayo. Ashidashi-p'i, chŏnŭn Han-guge shwipke iksuk'aejigo issŭmnida.
저, 저는 정말 괜찮아요. 아시다시피 저는 한국에 쉽게 익숙해지고 있습니다.

**Mr. Shim :** That's right. (*To the waiter*) Please bring us a small bottle of *soju* now, and two *naengmyon* afterwards.

**Waiter :** Yes, sir.

**Mr. Shim :** Two more portions of *pulgogi*, and another bottle of *soju*, please.

**Waiter :** Yes, sir. Right away, sir.

* * *

**Mr. Kim :** Miss Williams, I'll treat you to lunch.
Can you go now?

**Miss Williams :** Oh, thank you Mr. Kim. Yes, I am ready. Where to?

**Mr. Kim :** Well, you can have a choice. If you like hot rice and soup we can go to the Myongdonggwan for *kom-tang*, and if you like *mandu* or *ttokkuk* we can try the restaurant across

S : Kŭrŏk'unyo. Soju chagŭn kŏt han pyŏng chigŭm kajyŏogo, chom hue naengmyŏn tu kŭrŭt kajyŏoseyo.
그렇군요. (웨이터에게) 소주 작은 것 한 병 지금 가져오고, 좀 후에 냉면 두 그릇 가져오세요.

W : Ne, arassŭmnida.
네, 알았습니다.

S : Pulgogi iinbun-gwa soju han pyŏng tŏ kajyŏoseyo.
불고기 이인분과 소주 한 병 더 가져오세요.

W : Ne, kot kajyŏogessŭmnida.
네, 곧 가져오겠습니다.

* * *

K : Williŏmjŭ yang, chega chŏmshimŭl naegessŭmnida. Chigŭm kal su issŏyo?
윌리엄즈 양, 제가 점심을 내겠습니다. 지금 갈 수 있어요?

W : Kamsahamnida, Kim sŏnsaengnim. Ne, kal su issŏyo. Ŏdiroyo?
감사합니다, 김 선생님. 네, 갈 수 있어요. 어디로요?

K : Choŭshin taero korŭseyo. Ttŭgŏun papkwa kugŭl choahashimyŏn Myŏngdonggwane komt'angŭl harŏ kago, manduna ttŏkkugŭl choahashimyŏn chŏgi kil kŏnnŏp'yŏne innŭn shiktange kadorok hajiyo.
좋으신 대로 고르세요. 뜨거운 밥과 국을 좋아하시면 명동관에 곰탕을 하러 가고, 만두나 떡국을 좋아하시면 저기 길 건너편에 있는 식당에 가도록 하지요.

the street there.

**Miss Williams :** I like *mandu* a lot.

**Mr. Kim :** O.K. Let's cross the street here. Watch out! That cyclist nearly hit us.

*(They take seat in the restaurant.)*

**Mr. Kim :** Now Miss Williams, do you want only *mandu* or *mandu mixed with ttongmandu?*

**Miss Williams :** I'd like *mandu mixed with ttongmandu*, please.

**Mr. Kim :** (*To the waitress*) One *ttongmandu* and one *kelbitang*, please.

Waitress : Would you buy your meal tickets first, please? That'll be 3,000 won, sir.

**Mr. Kim :** Here it is.

Waitress : Thank you, sir.

**Miss Williams :** What is *kalbitang*, Mr. Kim?

**W** : Chŏnŭn mandurŭl taedanhi choahaeyo.
저는 만두를 대단히 좋아해요.

**K** : Chossŭmnida. Yŏgisŏ kirŭl kŏnnŏpshida. Choshimhaeyo! Chŏ chajŏn-gŏ t'an saram urirŭl ch'il ppŏnhaenne!
좋습니다. 여기서 길을 건넙시다. 조심해요! 저 자전거 탄 사람 우리를 칠 뻔했네.

(그들은 식당에서 자리에 앉는다.)

**K** : Williŏmjŭ yang, mandurŭl tŭlgessŏyo, animyŏn ttŏngmandurŭl tŭlgessŏyo?
윌리엄즈 양, 만두를 들겠어요, 아니면 떡만두를 들겠어요?

**W** : Nanŭn ttŏngmandurŭl tŭlgessŏyo.
나는 떡만두를 들겠어요.

**K** : Ttŏngmandu hanawa kalbit'ang hana kajyŏoseyo.
(여종업원에게) 떡만두 하나와 갈비탕 하나 가져오세요.

**Wa**: Shikkwŏnŭl mŏnjŏ sa chushigessŏyo? Samch'ŏnwŏni toegessŭmnida.
식권을 먼저 사 주시겠어요?
삼천원이 되겠습니다.

**K** Yŏgi issŭmnida.
여기 있습니다.

**Wa**: Komapsŭmnida.
고맙습니다.

**W** : Kim sŏnsaengnim, kalbit'angi muŏshimnikka?
김 선생님, 갈비탕이 무엇입니까?

**Mr. Kim :** That's beef's rib soup served with rice.

It's one of my favorite dishes.

**Miss Williams :** That sounds tasty. I'll try that next time.

### 3. In the Tearoom

**Miss Chang :** Hello, Miss Wrice! It's nice to see you.

**Miss Wrice :** Hello, Miss Chang! It's been a long time since I've seen you.

**Miss Chang :** Yes, it has. Can we talk for a while over a cup of coffee?

**Miss Wrice :** Fine, I'm free just now. Let's go to that tearoom over there.

**Miss Chang :** O.K. It must be a newly opened one. I see wreaths of flowers on both sides of the entrance.

**K** : Kŭgŏsŭn sogalbikugeda pabŭl man kŏshimnida. Chega choahanŭn ŭmshigimnida.
그것은 소갈비국에다 밥을 만 것입니다. 제가 좋아하는 음식입니다.

**W** : Madissŭl kŏt kat'ŭndeyo.
Taŭme mŏgŏ pojyo.
맛있을 것 같은데요.
다음에 먹어 보죠.

## 3. 찻집에서

**C** : Annyŏnghaseyo, misŭ Raisŭ! Poepke toeŏ pan-gawŏyo.
안녕하세요, 미스 라이스! 뵙게 되어 반가워요.

**W** : Annyŏnghaseyo, Chang yang! Poeon chi chŏng-mal orae toeŏssŭmnida.
안녕하세요, 장 양! 뵈온 지 정말 오래 되었습니다.

**C** : Ne, kŭrŏk'unyo. Chamkkan k'ŏp'ina han chan tŭl-myŏnsŏ iyagi nanulkkayo?
네, 그렇군요. 잠깐 커피나 한 잔 들면서 이야기 나눌까요?

**W** : Choayo. Na chigŭm shigan issŏyo. Chŏgi chŏ ta-bange kapshida.
좋아요. 나 지금 시간 있어요. 저기 저 다방에 갑시다.

**C** : Kŭrŏpshida. I tabang saero yŏrŏtkunyo. Ipku yang-tchoge hwahwani innŭn kŏsŭl ponikkayo.
그럽시다. 이 다방 새로 열었군요. 입구 양쪽에 화환이 있는 것을 보니까요.

*(They enter the tearoom.)*

**Waitress :** Good afternoon. Please come this way.

*(They sit down.)*

**Miss Wrice :** It's a beautiful tearoom. The lamps and decorations are nice.

**Miss Chang :** The music is excellent, too. They must have good equipment.

**Waitress :** What would you like to drink?

**Miss Chang :** Miss Wrice, would you like coffee?

**Miss Wrice :** No, I'd rather have ginger tea. I like its hot taste.

**Miss Chang :** (*To the waitress*) One ginger and one coffee, please.

**Waitress :** All right.

(그들은 다방에 들어간다.)

Wa: Annyŏnghaseyo.
Iriro oseyo.
안녕하세요.
이리로 오세요.

(그들은 앉는다.)

W : I tabang arŭmdapkunyo.
Chŏndŭnggwa changshigi chossŭmnida.
이 다방 아름답군요.
전등과 장식이 좋습니다.

C : Ŭmakto hullyunghagunyo.
Ŭmhyang shisŏri choŭn-ga pomnida.
음악도 훌륭하군요.
음향 시설이 좋은가 봅니다.

Wa: Muŏsŭl mashigessŭmnikka?
무엇을 마시겠습니까?

C : Raisŭ yang, k'ŏp'i tŭlgessŏyo?
라이스양, 커피 들겠어요?

W : Anio. Saenggangch'arŭl tŭlgessŏyo. Nanŭn kŭ maeun masŭl choahaeyo.
아니오. 생강차를 들겠어요. 나는 그 매운 맛을 좋아해요.

C : Saenggangch'a han chan-gwa k'ŏp'i han chan chuseyo.
(여종업원에게) 생강차 한 잔과 커피 한 잔 주세요.

Wa: Arassŭmnida.
알았습니다.

# V. SHOPPING

## ☐ Useful Expressions

1. Would you like to go shopping with me?
2. Would you help me do some shopping?
3. How about Tongdaemun Market?
4. Please show me that vase.
5. How much is it?
6. I want to buy some shirts.
7. Let me take a look at it.
8. Give me two boxes of strawberries.
9. How much are there all together?
10. Wrap them up, please.
11. I'd like to pick out a gift for my friend.
12. It is cheap.

# V. 쇼 핑

## □ 많이 쓰는 표현

1. Chŏwa kach'i syop'ing haro kashiryŏmnikka?
   저와 같이 쇼핑 하러 가시렵니까?
2. Syop'ing hanŭn kŏt chom towa chushigessŭmnikka?
   쇼핑 하는 것 좀 도와 주시겠습니까?
3. Tongdaemun shijangŭn ŏttŏseyo?
   동대문 시장은 어떠세요?
4. Chŏ hwabyŏngŭl poyŏ chuseyo.
   저 화병을 보여 주세요.
5. Ŏlmaimnikka? 얼마입니까?
6. Syassŭ chom sago ship'ŭndeyo.
   샤쓰 좀 사고 싶은데요.
7. Chom popshida. 좀 봅시다.
8. Ttalgi tu sangja chuseyo.
   딸기 두 상자 주세요.
9. Ta ŏlmaimnikka?
   다 얼마입니까?
10. Ssa chushipshio.
    싸 주십시오.
11. Ch'in-gu chul sŏnmurŭl hana korŭgo ship'ŭndeyo.
    친구 줄 선물을 하나 고르고 싶은데요.
12. Ssamnida.
    쌉니다.

13. It is not too expensive.

14. It is too expensive.

15. I like this one.

16. I don't like this one.

17. This is tax free.

    Can you make it a little cheaper?

18. I'd like a receipt, please.

19. We have fixed prices.

## 1. At a Gift Shop

**Miss Jones :** I would like to buy one of those dolls on the shelf.

**Salesgirl :** Here they are.

**Miss Jones :** This one looks very pretty. How much is it?

**Salesgirl :** That's 6,000 won.

13. Kŭrŏk'e pissaji anssŭmnida.
그렇게 비싸지 않습니다.
14. Nŏmu pissamnida.
너무 비쌉니다.
15. Igŏshi chossŭmnida.
이것이 좋습니다.
16. Igŏsŭn shirŏyo.
이것은 싫어요.
17. Kŭgŏsŭn myŏnsep'umimnida.
그것은 면세품입니다.
Chom ssage hal su issŏyo?
좀 싸게 할 수 있어요?
18. Yŏngsujŭngŭl hae chushipshio.
영수증을 해 주십시오.
19. Chŏngch'al kagyŏgimnida.
정찰 가격입니다.

## 1. 선물 가게에서

J : Chŏ sŏnbanŭi inhyŏngŭl hana sago shipsŭmnida.
저 선반의 인형을 하나 사고 싶습니다.
S : Yŏgi issŭmnida.
여기 있습니다.
J : Igŏsŭn ch'am kwiyŏpsŭmnida. Ŏlmajyo?
이것은 참 귀엽습니다.
얼마죠?
S : Yukch'ŏnwŏnimnida.
육천원입니다.

**Miss Jones :** That's not bad. How about this one?

**Salesgirl :** That's 7,000 won. It's a good buy.

**Miss Jones :** All right, I'll take it.

## 2. At a Jeweler's Store

**Miss Jones :** I want to see that amethyst ring in the middle.

**Salesgirl :** Do you mean this one?

**Miss Jones :** No, the one on the right.

**Salesgirl :** Here it is.

**Miss Jones :** Oh, this one is beautiful.
But, it is a little tight.
Don't you have a little larger one?

**Salesgirl :** Wait a second. Try this one.

**Miss Jones :** I think this one fits all right.
How much is it?

J : Kwaench'ank'unyo. Igŏsŭn ŏlmajyo?
괜찮군요. 이것은 얼마죠?

S : Kŭgŏsŭn ch'ilch'ŏnwŏnimnida. Kapshi kwaench'anssŭmnida.
그것은 칠천원입니다. 값이 괜찮습니다.

J : Choayo. Igŏsŭl sajyo.
좋아요. 이것을 사죠.

## 2. 귀금속상에서

J : Chŏ kaunde innŭn chasujŏng panji poyŏ chuseyo.
저 가운데 있는 자수정 반지 보여 주세요.

S : Igŏt marimnikka?
이것 말입니까?

J : Anio. Kŭ orŭnp'yŏnŭi kŏt marimnida.
아니오. 그 오른편의 것 말입니다.

S : Yŏgi issŭmnida.
여기 있습니다.

J : Ayu, igŏt yeppŭgunyo. Kŭrŏnde chom chagŭndeyo. Chom tŏ k'ŭn kŏt ŏpsŏyo?
아유, 이것 예쁘군요. 그런데 좀 작은데요. 좀 더 큰 것 없어요?

S : Chamkkan kidariseyo. Igŏt kkiŏ poseyo.
잠깐 기다리세요.
이것 끼어 보세요.

J : Igŏsŭn chal majayo. Ŏlmajyo?
이것은 잘 맞아요. 얼마죠?

**Salesgirl :** 15,000 won, Miss.

**Miss Jones :** Fine, I'll take it.

### 3. At a Silk Shop

**Miss Jones :** Please show me that green silk over there.

**Attendant :** Do you mean this?

**Miss Jones :** Yes, and the one under it, too.

**Attendant :** Here you are.

**Miss Jones :** I like this shade. How much is it a yard?

**Attendant :** It is 17,000 won a yard.

**Miss Jones :** I'd like a Korean dress for myself. Would 5 yards be enough for that?

**Attendant** That'll certainly be enough, Miss.

**Miss Jones :** Then, 5 yards, please.

S : Manoch'ŏnwŏnimnida
만오천원입니다.

J : Choayo. Igŏt sajyo.
좋아요. 이것 사죠.

## 3. 옷감집에서

J : Chŏgi innŭn yŏndusaek shilk'ŭrŭl chom poyŏ chuseyo.
저기 있는 연두색 실크를 좀 보여 주세요.

A : Igŏt malssŭmimnikka?
이것 말씀입니까?

J : Ne, kŭ mit'e innŭn kŏtto poyo chuseyo.
네. 그 밑에 있는 것도 보여 주세요.

A : Yŏgi issŭmnida.
여기 있습니다.

J : I saekkari choayo.
이 색깔이 좋아요.
Han ma-e ŏlmaimnikka?
한 마에 얼마입니까?

A : Han ma-e manch'ilchŏnwŏnimnida.
한 마에 만칠천원입니다.

J : Chega hanbogŭl mach'uryŏnŭndeyo, tasŏt ma-myŏn toemnikka?
제가 한복을 맞추려는데요. 다섯 마면 됩니까?

A : Aju nŏngnŏk'amnida, agassi.
아주 넉넉합니다, 아가씨.

J : Kŭrŏm tasŏt ma chuseyo. 그럼 다섯 마 주세요.

**Attendant :** All right, Miss.

## 4. At a Bookstore

**Mr. Johnson :** Do you have a tour guide of Korea?

**Clerk :** Yes, we do. Here is one.

**Mr. Johnson :** It is just what I wanted. How much is it?

**Clerk :** It's 4,000 won, sir. Do you need anything else? We have a very good map of Seoul, too.

**Mr. Johnson :** All right. Let me take a look at it.

**Clerk :** Here it is.

**Mr. Johnson :** It's fine. How much is it?

**Clerk :** It's only 1,000 won.

**Mr. Johnson :** O.K. I'll take it, too. Now,

A : Ne, kŭrŏk'e hajyo.
네, 그렇게 하죠.

## 4. 책방에서

J : Han-guk yŏhaeng annaesŏ issŭmnikka?
한국 여행 안내서 있습니까?

C : Ne, issŭmnida.
Yŏgi issŏyo.
네, 있습니다.
여기 있어요.

J : Igŏshi paro naega wŏnhadŏn kŏyeyo.
Ŏlmajyo?
이것이 바로 내가 원하던 거예요.
얼마죠?

C : Sach'ŏnwŏnimnida. Tto tarŭn kŏt p'iryohashimnikka? Sŏul chidodo choŭn kŏshi issŭmnida.
사천원입니다. 또 다른 것 필요하십니까? 서울 지도도 좋은 것이 있습니다.

J : Ne, kŭgŏt chom popshida.
네, 그것 좀 봅시다.

C : Yŏgi issŭmnida.
여기 있습니다.

J : Chok'unyo. Ŏlmajyo?
좋군요. 얼마죠?

C : Ch'ŏnwŏnbakke an hamnida.
천원밖에 안 합니다.

J : Chossŭmnida. Kŭgŏtto sajyo. Ŏlmaga toegessŭm-

how much will that be?

**Clerk :** That will be 5,000 won, sir.

**Mr. Johnson :** Here it is.

**Clerk :** Thank you very much.
Please come again.

(*Mr. Smith is walking around the streets of Seoul.*)

**Mr. Smith :** Where can I get a tourist map of Korea?

**A Passer-by :** You can get one in any big bookstore in town.

**Mr. Simth :** Where is the nearest one?

**A Passer-by :** Go down that road and turn left at the second traffic light and will find several bookstores on your left.

**Mr. Smith :** Thank you very much.

**A Passer-by :** Don't mention it.

nikka?
좋습니다. 그것도 사죠. 얼마가 되겠습니까?

C : Och'ŏnwŏni toegessŭmnida.
오천원이 되겠습니다.

J : Yŏgi issŭmnida.
여기 있습니다.

C : Taedanhi kamsahamnida.
Tto oshipshio.
대단히 감사합니다.
또 오십시오.

(스미드 씨는 서울의 시가를 걷고 있다)

S : Han-guk kwan-gwang chidorŭl ŏdiesŏ sal su issŭmnikka?
한국 관광 지도를 어디에서 살 수 있습니까?

P : Shinae k'ŭn ch'aekpangimyŏn ŏdiesŏdŭnji kuhal su issŭmnida.
시내 큰 책방이면 어디에서든지 구할 수 있습니다.

S : Ŏdiga cheil kakkaun koshimnikka?
어디가 제일 가까운 곳입니까?

P : Chŏ kirŭl naeryŏgadaga tultchaepŏn shinhodŭng-esŏ oentchogŭro torasŏ kashimyŏn, oentchoge ch'aekpangi yŏrŏt poimnida.
저 길을 내려가다가 둘째번 신호등에서 왼쪽으로 돌아서 가시면, 왼쪽에 책방이 여럿 보입니다.

S : Taedanhi kamsahamnida.
대단히 감사합니다.

P : Ch'ŏnmaneyo.
천만에요.

## 5. At a Department Store

**Mr. James :** I'm looking for some white shirts, please.

**Salesgirl :** What size do you take, sir?

**Mr. James :** I take $15\frac{1}{2}$ and 33.

**Salesgirl :** Just a second, please.

(*She brings out several shirts.*)

Well, this one is 19,000 won and these two are 17,500 won each.

**Mr. James :** I see. This 19,000 won shirt looks fine.

What kind of material is this?

**Salesgirl :** It is a new type of synthetic material.

It feels very soft. There's no static, sir.

**Mr. James :** All right. I'll take two of this

## 5. 백화점에서

J : Hŭin syassŭrŭl saryŏgo hanŭndeyo.
흰 샤쓰를 사려고 하는데요.

S : Ŏttŏn saijŭrŭl wŏnhamnikka?
어떤 사이즈를 원합니까?

J : Chŏnŭn shibo pane samshipsamŭl ipsŭmnida.
저는 십오 반에 삼십삼을 입습니다.

S : Chamkkanman kidaryŏ chuseyo.
잠깐만 기다려 주세요.

(샤쓰를 몇 개 가져온다)

Igŏsŭn mankuch'ŏnwŏnigo, i tukaenŭn kakkak manch'ilch'ŏnobaegwŏnssigimnida.
이것은 만구천원이고, 이 두개는 각각 만칠천오백원씩 입니다.

J : Arassŭmnida.
I mankuch'ŏnwŏntchariga choa poimmida.
Igŏsŭn musŭn kamijyo?
알았읍니다.
이 만구천원짜리가 좋아 보입니다.
이것은 무슨 감이죠?

S : Igŏsŭn saero naon hapsŏng sŏmyuimnida. Aju pudŭrŏpsŭmnida.
Chŏngjŏn-giga an irŏnamnida.
이것은 새로 나온 합성 섬유입니다. 아주 부드럽습니다.
정전기가 안 일어납니다.

J : Chossŭmnida. Irŏn kŏt tu kae sagessŭmnida.

kind, please.

**Salesgirl :** Yes, sir. Do you need anything else?

**Mr. James :** No, just those two shirts, please.

**Salesgirl :** All right, sir. I'll wrap them up right away.

### 6. At the Handbag Section

(*At the information booth*)

**Girl :** May I help you?

**Miss White :** Where can I find handbags?

**Girl :** You will find them on the 3rd floor on your left as you go up the escalator.

**Miss White :** Thank you.

**Girl :** You're welcome.

* * *

(*At the handbag section*)

좋습니다. 이런 것 두 개 사겠습니다.

S : Ne, tto tarŭn kŏt p'iryohashimnikka?
네, 또 다른 것 필요하십니까?

J : Anio.
I syassŭ tu changimyŏn toemnida.
아니오.
이 샤쓰 두 장이면 됩니다.

S : Arassŭmnida. Kot ssa tŭrigessŭmnida.
알았습니다. 곧 싸 드리겠습니다.

## 6. 핸드백 부에서

(안내대에서)

G : Towa tŭrilkkayo?
도와 드릴까요?

W : Ŏdisŏ haendŭbaegŭl sal su itchyo?
어디서 핸드백을 살 수 있죠?

G : Esŭk'ŏlleit'ŏro ollagashimyŏn samch'ŭng oentchoge issŭmnida.
에스컬레이터로 올라가시면 삼층 왼쪽에 있습니다.

W : Kamsahamnida.
감사합니다.

G : Ch'ŏnmaneyo.
천만에요.

* * *

(핸드백 부에서)

**Salesgirl :** Good afternoon, Miss. May I help you?

**Miss White :** Yes, I would like to pick out a handbag for my mother.

**Salesgirl :** How about those on the rack?

**Miss White :** They seem fine. I want to see that one on the right.

**Salesgirl :** You mean the brown one?

**Miss White :** No, the black one beside it.

**Salesgirl :** All right.

**Miss White :** Oh, this is wonderful.
How much is it?

**Salesgirl :** It's 45,000 won, Miss.

**Miss White :** Oh, dear! That's too expensive.

**Salesgirl :** Then, how about this one? It is equally good, but a little cheaper.
It's only 31,000 won.

S : Ŏsŏ oshipshio. Towa tŭrilkkayo?
어서 오십시오. 도와 드릴까요?

W : Ne, che ŏmŏnikke tŭril haendubaegŭl hana korŭryŏnŭndeyo.
네, 제 어머니께 드릴 핸드백을 하나 고르려는데요.

S : I sŏnban wie innŭn kŏttŭrŭn ŏttŏssŭmnikka?
이 선반 위에 있는 것들은 어떻습니까?

W : Pogi kwaench'anŭndeyo.
Orŭntchoge innŭn kŏsŭl poyŏ chuseyo.
보기 괜찮은데요.
오른쪽에 있는 것을 보여 주세요.

S : I kalsaek kŏt marimnikka?
이 갈색 것 말입니까?

W : Anio. Kŭ yŏp'e innŭn kŏmŭn kŏshiyo.
아니오. 그 옆에 있는 검은 것이요.

S : Ne, arassŭmnida.
네, 알았습니다.

W : Ayu, mŏdinnŭndeyo. Ŏlmayeyo?
아유, 멋있는데요. 얼마예요?

S : Samanoch'ŏnwŏnimnida.
사만오천원입니다.

W : Ŏmŏna, nŏmu pissagunyo.
어머나, 너무 비싸군요.

S : Kŭrŏm igŏsŭn ŏttaeyo? Igŏsŭn mach'an-gajiro choŭn kŏshinde ssamnida. Sammanch'ŏnwŏnbakke an haeyo.
그럼, 이것은 어때요? 이것은 마찬가지로 좋은 것인데 쌉니다. 삼만천원밖에 안 해요.

**Miss White** : Hum. It's not bad. All right, I'll take it.

**Salesgirl** : I'll wrap it up for you.

But if you'd like it gift-wrapped, there's a wrapping service on the first floor.

**Miss White** : Thank you. Here's the money.

**Salesgirl** : Thank you. Please come again.

## 7. At a Souvenir Shop

**Salesclerk** : Please come in. What would you like, sir?

**Mr. Dean** : Well, I'd like some typical Korean souvenir. Not, too big, nor too expensive.

**Salesclerk** : Well, then, come this way, please. We have a variety of brassware over here.

W : Ŭm, kwaench'ank'unyo. Chossŭmnida. Kŭgŏt sagessŏyo.
음, 괜찮군요. 좋습니다. 그것 사겠어요.

S : P'ojanghae tŭrigessŭmnida. Kŭrŏnde, sŏnmulyong p'ojangŭl wŏnhashimyŏn ilch'ŭnge p'ojangbuga issŭmnida.
포장해 드리겠습니다. 그런데, 선물용 포장을 원하시면 일층에 포장부가 있습니다.

W : Kamsahamnida. Yŏgi ton issŭmnida.
감사합니다. 여기 돈 있습니다.

S : Kamsahamnida. Tto oshipshio.
감사합니다. 또 오십시오.

## 7. 기념품상에서

S : Ŏsŏ oshipshio.
Muŏsŭl sashiryŏmnikka?
어서 오십시오.
무엇을 사시렵니까?

D : Kŭlsseyo. Chŏnhyŏngjŏgin Han-guk kinyŏmp'umŭl sago ship'ŭndeyo. Nŏmu k'ŭjido ank'o nŏmu pissajido anŭn kŏsŭroyo.
글쎄요. 전형적인 한국 기념품을 사고 싶은데요. 너무 크지도 않고 너무 비싸지도 않은 것으로요.

S : Kŭrŏshimyŏn itchogŭro oshipshio. Yŏgi yugi chep'umi yŏrŏ chongnyu issŭmnida.
그러시면 이쪽으로 오십시오. 여기 유기 제품이 여러 종류 있습니다.

**Mr. Dean :** Good. I think I can find something here.

How much is this ash tray?

**Salesclerk :** That's 8,500 won, sir.

**Mr. Dean :** Hum. That's not bad. How much is that one?

**Salesclerk :** That's 5,000 won, sir. It's much smaller but it's very pretty.

**Mr. Dean :** I think so, too. Well, I'll take three of them, please. Wrap each of them separately. I've got many friends back home.

**Salesclerk :** Yes, sir. Would you like to pick out something else?

**Mr. Dean :** Let me see,

I don't know.

**Salesclerk :** How about these bamboo pipes or those Korean fans?

D : Choayo. Yŏgisŏ chom korŭl su issŭl kŏt katkun-yo.
I chaettŏri ŏlmaimnikka?
좋아요. 여기서 좀 고를 수 있을 것 같군요.
이 재떨이 얼마입니까?

S : Kŭgŏsŭn palch'ŏnobaewŏnimnida.
그것은 팔천오백원입니다.

D : Ŭm, kŭgŏt kwaench'ank'unyo.
Chŏgŏsŭn ŏlmajyo?
음, 그것 괜찮군요.
저것은 얼마죠?

S : Chŏgŏsŭn och'ŏnwŏnimnida.
Aju chakchiman taedanhi yeppŭmnida.
저것은 오천원입니다.
아주 작지만 대단히 예쁩니다.

D : Chŏdo kŭrŏk'e saenggak'amnida. Kŭrŏm chŏgŏt se kaerŭl sagessŭmnida. Kakkak ttaro p'ojanghae chushijiyo. Kohyange ch'in-guga yŏrŏshinikkayo.
저도 그렇게 생각합니다. 그럼 저것 세 개를 사겠습니다. 각각 따로 포장해 주시지요. 고향에 친구가 여럿이니까요.

S : Ne, tto tarŭn kŏt korŭshil kŏt ŏpsŭseyo?
네, 또 다른 것 고르실 것 없으세요?

D : Kŭlsseyo, morŭgennŭndeyo.
글쎄요, 모르겠는데요.

S : I taenamu tambaettaena Han-guk puch'aenŭn ŏttŏseyo?
이 대나무 담뱃대나 한국 부채는 어떠세요?

**Mr. Dean :** They seem to be a good idea. How much are they?

**Salesclerk :** The longer pipes are 3,500 won each and the shorter ones are 2,000 won, sir. And these Korean Taeguk fans are 2,000 won each.

**Mr. Dean :** They are not expensive at all. Well, let me have two of those short pipes and five fans, please.

**Salesclerk :** Yes, sir. Should I wrap them separately, also?

**Mr. Dean :** No, there's no need to. How much are all these?

**Salesclerk :** The total will be 27,000 won, sir.

**Mr. Dean :** Here's a 100,000 won bill.

**Salesclerk :** Thank you.
Here's your change. Please come back again. Good-bye.

D : Kŭgŏt ch'am choŭn saenggagigunyo. Ólmaimnikka?
그것 참 좋은 생각이군요. 얼마입니까?

S : Kin tambaettaenŭn samch'ŏnobaegwŏnigo, tchalbŭn kŏsŭn ich'ŏnwŏnimnida. Kŭrigo i t'aegŭk puch'aenŭn ich'ŏnwŏnimnida.
긴 담뱃대는 삼천오백원이고, 짧은 것은 이천원입니다. 그리고 이 태극 부채는 이천원입니다

D : Pyŏllo pissaji ank'unyo. Kŭrŏm, i tchalbŭn tambaettae tu kaewa puch'ae tasŏt kae chushipshio.
별로 비싸지 않군요. 그럼, 이 짧은 담뱃대 두 개와 부채 다섯 개 주십시오.

S : Ne, tto kakkak p'ojanghalkkayo?
네, 또 각각 포장할까요?

D : Anio. Kŭrŏl p'iryo ŏpsŏyo.
Modu ŏlmaimnikka?
아니오. 그럴 필요 없어요.
모두 얼마입니까?

S : Hapkyega imanch'ilch'ŏnwŏni toemnida.
합계가 이만칠천원이 됩니다.

D : Yŏgi sipmanwŏn sup'yo issŭmnida.
여기 십만원 수표 있습니다.

S : Kamsahamnida.
Kŏsŭrŭmton yŏgi issŭmnida.
Tto oseyo. Annyŏnghi kashipshio.
감사합니다.
거스름돈 여기 있습니다.
또 오세요. 안녕히 가십시오.

## 8. At the Curio Shop

**Dealer** : Good afternoon, Mr. Clark.

**Mr. Clark** : Good afternoon, Mr. Lee.

I come to settle on that chest I saw the other day.

**Dealer** : Yes, sir. Please have a seat here.

**Mr. Clark** : No, never mind.

I saw another chest just like that at Tongdaemun, and they only ask 550,000.

Can't you make your price a little less?

**Dealer** : Well, since you came again, I will ask you only 580,000 won. But remember Mr. Clark, ours is a genuine one and the most beautiful one.

**Mr. Clark** : I know. Well, agreed, Mr. Lee.

## 8. 골동품상에서

D : Annyŏnghashimnikka, Kŭllak'ŭ ssi.
안녕하십니까, 클라크 씨.

C : Annyŏnghaseyo, I sajangnim. Chŏne pon kŭ changŭl sagiro hago wassŭmnida.
안녕하세요, 이 사장님. 전에 본 그 장을 사기로 하고 왔습니다.

D : Ne, iriro anjŭshipshio.
네, 이리로 앉으십시오.

C : Kwaench'anssŭmnida. Chega Tongdaemunesŏ chŏgŏtkwa ttokkat'ŭn kŏsŭl poannŭnde, oshibomanwŏnbakke an haeyo. Kagyŏgŭl chom kkakkŭl su ŏpsŭlkkayo?
괜찮습니다. 제가 동대문에서 저것과 똑같은 것을 보았는데, 오십오만원밖에 안 해요. 가격을 좀 깎을 수 없을까요?

D : Chŏ, tashi oshigido haessŭni oshipp'almanwŏnman purŭgessŭmnida. Kŭrŏna K'ŭllak'ŭ ssi, uri kŏsŭn chintchaigo kajang arŭmdaun kŏshiranŭn kŏsŭl asyŏya hamnida.
저, 다시 오시기도 했으니 오십팔만원만 부르겠습니다. 그러나 클라크 씨, 우리 것은 진짜이고 가장 아름다운 것이라는 것을 아셔야 합니다.

C : Amnida. Kŭrŏm sagiro hajiyo. Onŭl chŏnyŏge chibŭro paedarhae chushipshio. Che kaein sup'yodo toegessŭmnikka?

Please send it to my house this evening.

Will my personal check do?

**Dealer :** No problem at all, sir.

By the way, Mr. Clark, I just got a beautiful stationary bureau. It's a 17th century piece.

I'm sure you'll like it.

Would you like to take a look at it?

**Mr. Clark :** Well, which one do you mean?

**Dealer :** This way, please. That small dark one behind the table.

**Mr. Clark :** Hum, that's beautiful. I'll drop by in two or three days. Good-bye.

**Dealer :** All right, sir. Good-bye.

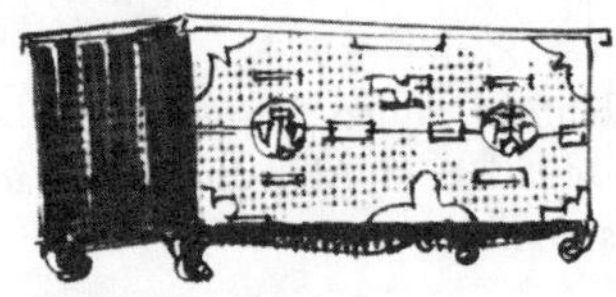

압니다. 그럼 사기로 하지요. 오늘 저녁에 집으로 배달 해 주십시오. 제 개인 수표로 되겠습니까?

D : Mullon kwaench'anssŭmnida. Kŭrŏnde K'ŭllak'ŭ ssi, mŏdinnŭn ch'aekchangi hana mak tŭrŏwassŭmnida. Shipch'il segi kŏshimnida. Ama maŭme tŭshilkŏmnida. Hanbŏn poshigessŭmnikka?

물론 괜찮습니다. 그런데 클라크 씨, 멋있는 책장이 하나 막 들어왔습니다. 십칠 세기 것입니다. 아마 마음에 드실 겁니다. 한번 보시겠습니까?

C : Kŭlsseyo. Ŏnŭ kŏt malssŭmimnikka?

글쎄요. 어느 것 말씀입니까?

D : Itchogŭro oshipshio. Chŏ ch'aeksang twie innŭn chakko kŏmŭn kŏt marimnida.

이쪽으로 오십시오. 저 책상 뒤에 있는 작고 검은 것 말입니다.

C : Ŭm, kŭgŏt ch'am chok'unyo. Isamil ane tashi tŭllŭgessŭmnida. Annyŏnghi kyeseyo.

음, 그것 참 좋군요. 이삼일 안에 다시 들르겠습니다. 안녕히 계세요.

D : Arassŭmnida. Annyŏnghi kashipshio.

알았습니다. 안녕히 가십시오.

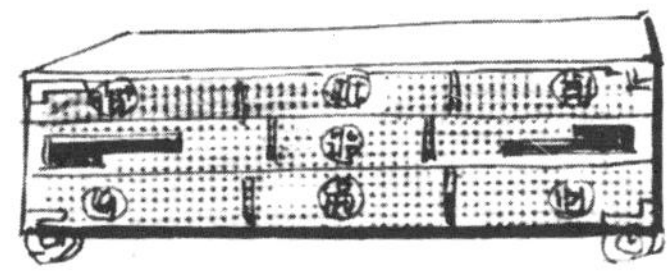

# VI. TELEPHONE

## ☐ Useful Expressions

1. May I use your telephone?
2. Where is a public telephone?
3. Is that Mr. Song's residence?
4. I'd like to talk to Mr. Lee, please.
5. He is not in just now.
6. When will he be back?
7. I'd like to leave a message.
8. Would you like to leave a message?
9. Just tell him that I called.
10. Please tell him to call me back as soon as possible.
11. Shall I have him call you?

# VI. 전 화

## □ 많이 쓰는 표현

1. Chŏnhwarŭl sayonghaedo toelkkayo?
   전화를 사용해도 될까요?
2. Kongjung chŏnhwaga ŏdie issŭmnikka?
   공중 전화가 어디에 있습니까?
3. Song sŏnsaengnim taegimnikka?
   송 선생님 댁입니까?
4. I sŏnsaengnimŭl pakkwŏ chushigessŭmnikka?
   이 선생님을 바꿔 주시겠습니까?
5. Chigŭm i kose ŏpsŭmnida.
   지금 이 곳에 없습니다.
6. Ŏnje toraomnikka?
   언제 돌아옵니까?
7. Chŏnhal mari issŭmnida.
   전할 말이 있습니다.
8. Malssŭm chom chŏnhae chushigessŭmnikka?
   말씀 좀 전해 주시겠습니까?
9. Chega chŏnhwa kŏrŏttago illŏ chuseyo.
   제가 전화 걸었다고 일러 주세요.
10. Toedorok ppalli chŏege chŏnhwahae tallago malssŭmhae chuseyo.
    되도록 빨리 저에게 전화해 달라고 말씀해 주세요.
11. Kŭege chŏnhwa kŏllago marhalkkayo?
    그에게 전화 걸라고 말할까요?

12. Who's calling, please?
13. What is your telephone number?
14. The line is busy. Please wait a little.
15. I'm sorry, you have the wrong number.
16. I'll call again.
17. Thank you for calling.
18. Hello, is this the long distance call?
19. Hello, is this the overseas service?
20. I'd like to call New York, please.

## 1. To the Office

**Secretary** : Hello, Mr. Song's office.

**Mr. Smith** : Hello, I'd like to talk to Mr. Song, please.

**Secretary** : Who shall I say is calling?

**Mr. Smith** : This is William Smith, his friend.

12. Nugushimnikka? 누구십니까?
13. Chŏnhwa pŏnhoga myŏt pŏnimnikka?
전화 번호가 몇 번입니까?
14. T'onghwajungimnida. Chamkkan kidaryŏ chushipshio.
통화중입니다. 잠깐 기다려 주십시오.
15. Mianhamnidaman chalmot kŏsyŏssŭmnida.
미안합니다만 잘못 거셨습니다.
16. Tashi chŏnhwahagessŭmnida.
다시 전화하겠습니다.
17. Chŏnhwa chusyŏsŏ kamsahamnida.
전화 주셔서 감사합니다.
18. Yŏboseyo. Shioe chŏnhwaimnikka?
여보세요. 시외 전화입니까?
19. Yŏboseyo. Kukche chŏnhwaimnikka?
여보세요. 국제 전화입니까?
20. Nyuyok'ŭ put'ak'amnida.
뉴요크 부탁합니다.

## 1. 사무실에 걸 때

S : Yŏboseyo, misŭt'ŏ Song samushirimnida.
여보세요, 미스터 송 사무실입니다.

Sm: Yŏboseyo, misŭt'ŏ Songŭl pakkwŏ chushigessŭmnikka?
여보세요, 미스터 송을 바꿔 주시겠습니까?

S : Nugushirago halkkayo? 누구시라고 할까요?

Sm: Ch'ingu Williŏm Sŭmidŭimnida.
친구 윌리엄 스미드입니다.

**Secretary** : One moment, please.

*   *   *

**Mr. Song** : Hello. Mr. Smith, how are you?

**Mr. Smith** : Fine, thank you. And you?

**Mr. Song** : I'm fine, too.

**Mr. Smith** : I have something I'd like to talk to you about.

Can you meet me sometime tomorrow?

**Mr. Song** : Of course. How about two o'clock in the afternoon?

**Mr. Smith** : That'll be fine.

Then, I'll see you tomorrow at two at your office.

**Mr. Song** : All right. Mr. Smith.

**Mr. Smith** : Thank you, Mr. Song. Good-bye.

S : Chamkkanmanyo.
잠깐만요.

* * *

So : Yŏboseyo. Sŭmidŭ ssi, annyŏnghaseyo?
여보세요. 스미드 씨, 안녕하세요?

Sm: Ne, chal issŭmnida.
Taegŭn ŏttŏseyo?
네, 잘 있습니다.
댁은 어떠세요?

So : Chŏdo chal issŭmnida.
저도 잘 있습니다.

Sm: Tangshinege iyagihago ship'ŭn kŏshi issŭmnida. Naeil ŏnje manna poel su issŭmnikka?
당신에게 이야기하고 싶은 것이 있습니다. 내일 언제 만나 뵐 수 있습니까?

So : Mullonijyo. Ohu tushiga ottŏssŭmnikka?
물론이죠. 오후 두 시가 어떻습니까?

Sm: Kŭ shigani chok'etkunyo. Kŭrŏm tushie samushiresŏ poepkessŭmnida.
그 시간이 좋겠군요. 그럼 두시에 사무실에서 뵙겠습니다.

So : Arassŭmnida. Sŭmidŭ ssi.
알았습니다. 스미드 씨.

Sm: Kamsahamnida. Song sŏnsaengnim. Annyŏnghi kyeshipshio.
감사합니다. 송 선생님. 안녕히 계십시오.

**Mr. Song :** Good-bye.

## 2. To the House

**Mrs. Johnson :** I'd like to talk to Mr. Park, please.

**Voice :** I'm sorry, he's not in right now.

Who's calling, please?

**Mrs. Johnson :** This is Mrs. Johnson. When would he be back?

**Voice :** He may be back late in the afternoon.

Would you like to leave a messgae?

**Mrs. Johnson :** Just tell him that I called.

Good-bye.

**Voice :** Good-bye.

## 3. Samil Company

**Operator :** Samil Company.

So : Annyŏnghi kyeseyo.
안녕히 계세요.

## 2. 집으로 걸 때

J : Pak sŏnsaengnimŭl pakkwŏ chushigessŭmnikka?
박 선생님을 바꿔 주시겠습니까?

V : Mianhamnida. Chigŭm yŏgie ŏpsŭmnida. Nugushijyo?
미안합니다. 지금 여기에 없습니다. 누구시죠?

J : Chonsŭnimnida.
Ŏnje toraomnikka?
존슨입니다.
언제 돌아옵니까?

V : Ohu nŭtke toraol kŏshimnida.
Chŏnhal malssŭmi issŭmnikka?
오후 늦게 돌아올 것입니다.
전할 말씀이 있습니까?

J : Chega chŏnhwa kŏrŏttagoman haseyo.
Annyŏnghi kyeshipshio.
제가 전화 걸었다고만 하세요. 안녕히 계십시오.

V : Annyŏnghi kyeseyo.
안녕히 계세요.

## 3. 삼일 상사

O : Samil sangsaimnida.
삼일 상사입니다.

**Mr. Green :** President Im, please.

**Operator :** One moment, please.

**Secretary :** President Im's office.

**Mr. Green :** This is Jack Green. May I speak to President Im, please?

**Secretary :** I'm sorry. He's in conference right now.

Would you call back about an hour later?

**Mr. Green :** Yes, I will. Thank you. Good-bye.

**Secretary :** Good-bye.

### 4. Making an Appointment

**Miss. Dupont :** Hello. Is that 337–4598?

**Voice :** Yes, it is.

**Miss Dupont :** I'd like to talk to Miss Lee Yong Hwa, please.

G : Im hoejangnim put'ak'amnida.
임 회장님 부탁합니다.

O : Chamkkanman kidariseyo.
잠깐만 기다리세요.

S : Im hoejangshirimnida.
임 회장실입니다.

G : Chaek Kŭrinimnida. Im hoejangnim put'ak'amnida.
잭 그린입니다. 임 회장님 부탁합니다.

S : Mianhamnida. Chigŭm hoeŭi chungishindeyo. Han shigan hue tashi kŏrŏ chushigessŭmnikka?
미안합니다. 지금 회의 중이신데요. 한 시간 후에 다시 걸어 주시겠습니까?

G : Ne, kŭrŏk'e hagessŭmnida.
Annyŏnghi kyeshipshio.
네, 그렇게 하겠습니다.
안녕히 계십시오.

S : Annyŏnghi kyeseyo.
안녕히 계세요.

## 4. 약속할 때

D : Yŏboseyo. samsamch'ire saogup'arimnikka?
여보세요, 삼삼칠에 사오구팔입니까?

V : Ne, kŭrŏssŭmnida.
네, 그렇습니다.

D : I Yŏnghwa yangŭl pakkwŏ chushigessŏyo?
이 영화 양을 바꿔 주시겠어요?

**Voice :** One moment, please.

* * *

**Miss Lee :** Hello.

**Miss Dupont :** Hello, Yong Hwa? This is Jane.

**Miss Lee :** Hi! Jane. How are you?

**Miss Dupont :** Fine. Listen! How about a picnic tomorrow?

A couple of friends are going, and I'd like you to come.

**Miss Lee :** Thank you, Jane. Where are we going?

**Miss Dupont :** To the river near Paltang Dam.

**Miss Lee :** That's wonderful! What time do we leave?

**Miss Dupont :** At 10 in the morning.

Will that be all right?

V : Chamkkan kidarishipshio.
잠깐 기다리십시오.

* * *

L : Yŏboseyo.
여보세요.

D : Yŏboseyo, Yŏnghwa yangiseyo? Cheinieyo.
여보세요, 영화 양이세요? 제인이에요.

L : Chein! Annyŏnghaseyo?
제인! 안녕하세요?

D : Chal issŭmnida. Nae mal chom tŭrŏ pwayo. Nae-il sop'ung kanŭn kŏ ŏttaeyo?
Myŏt ch'in-guwa karyŏnŭnde tangshindo kassŭmyŏn chok'enneyo.
잘 있습니다. 내 말 좀 들어 봐요. 내일 소풍 가는 거 어때요?
몇 친구와 가려는데 당신도 갔으면 좋겠네요.

L : Kamsahamnida, Chein. Ŏdiro kanayo?
감사합니다, 제인. 어디로 가나요?

D : P'altang taem kŭnch'ŏ kangŭroyo.
팔당 댐 근처 강으로요.

L : Kŭgŏt ch'am mŏditkunyo.
Myŏt shie ttŏnayo?
그것 참 멋있군요!
몇 시에 떠나요?

D : Ach'im yŏlshieyo. Kwaench'anayo?
아침 열시에요. 괜찮아요?

**Miss Lee :** Sure.

**Miss Dupont :** Good. I'll see you tomorrow at 10.

Good-bye.

**Miss Lee :** Good-bye.

## 5. Reservation

**Mr. Smith :** Hello. Is that Korea Travel Service?

**Voice :** No, you have the wrong number.

**Mr. Smith :** Isn't that 275–8963?

**Voice :** No, this is 8962.

**Mr. Smith :** I'm sorry.

**Voice :** That's all right.

* * *

**Mr. Smith :** Hello.

**Clerk :** Good afternoon. Korea Travel Service.

L : Kŭrŏmyo.
그럼요.
D : Choayo. Kŭrŏm naeil yŏlshie mannayo. Annyŏng.
좋아요. 그럼 내일 열시에 만나요. 안녕.
L : Annyŏng. 안녕.

## 5. 예 약

S : Yŏboseyo, Han-guk yŏhaengsaimnikka?
여보세요, 한국 여행사입니까?
V : Animnida. Chalmot kŏsyŏssŭmnida.
아닙니다. 잘못 거셨습니다.
S : Ich'iro-e p'alguyuksam animnikka?
이칠오에 팔구육삼 아닙니까?
V : Animnida. P'alguyugiimnida.
아닙니다. 팔구육이입니다.
S : Mianhamnida.
미안합니다.
V : Kwaench'anssŭmnida.
괜찮습니다.

* * *

S : Yŏboseyo.
여보세요.
C : Annyŏnghashimnikka. Han-guk yŏhaengsaimnida.
안녕하십니까, 한국 여행사입니다.

**Mr. Smith :** I'd like to reserve a round-trip ticket to Cheju-do and a hotel room for three nights, please.

**Clerk :** All right, sir. When would you like to leave?

**Mr. Smith :** I'd like to leave next Friday afternoon.

**Clerk :** Yes, sir. May I have your name and phone number, please?

**Mr. Smith :** My name is John Smith, and my home phone number is 556–0506.

**Clerk :** Thank you. I'll call you as soon as your reservation is made.

**Mr. Smith :** Thank you. Good-bye.

**Clerk :** Good-bye.

S : Chejudohaeng wangbokp'yowa sahŭl pam mŏmul hot'el pang yeyagŭl haryŏmnida.
제주도행 왕복표와 사흘 밤 머물 호텔 방 예약을 하렵니다.

C : Arassŭmnida.
Ŏnje ttŏnashigessŭmnikka?
알았습니다.
언제 떠나시겠습니까?

S : Taŭm kŭmyoil ohue ttŏnaryŏmnida.
다음 금요일 오후에 떠나렵니다.

C : Ne, sŏnghamgwa chŏnhwa pŏnhorŭl allyŏ chushipshio.
네, 성함과 전화 번호를 알려 주십시오.

S : Nae irŭmŭn chon Sŭmidŭigo, chŏnhwa pŏnhonŭn ooyuge yŏngoyongyugimnida.
내 이름은 존 스미드이고, 전화 번호는 오오육에 영오영육입니다.

C : Kamsahamnida. Yeyagi toemyŏn kot chŏnhwahagessŭmnida.
감사합니다. 예약이 되면 곧 전화하겠습니다.

S : Kamsahamnida. Annyŏnghi kyeshipshio.
감사합니다. 안녕히 계십시오.

C : Annyŏnghi kyeshipshio.
안녕히 계십시오.

# VII. AT THE POST OFFICE

## ☐ Useful Expressions

1. Where's the nearest post office (mail box)?
2. Please give me five seventy won stamps.
3. Please weigh this letter.
4. I would like to send these letters air mail.
5. I want to send this package by surface mail.
6. How much postage do I have to put on?
7. I want to send this letter by registered post (mail).
8. How soon will it be delivered?
9. How long will it take to get there?
10. Please fill in this slip (form).

# VII. 우체국에서

## □ 많이 쓰는 표현

1. Kajang kakkaun uch'eguk(uch'et'ong) i ŏdiissŭmnikka?
   가장 가까운 우체국(우체통)이 어디 있습니까?
2. Ch'ilshibwŏntchari up'yo tasŏt chang chushipshio.
   칠십원짜리 우표 다섯 장 주십시오.
3. I p'yŏnji tara chuseyo.
   이 편지 달아 주세요.
4. I p'yŏnjirŭl hanggong up'yŏnŭro puch'iryŏmnida.
   이 편지를 항공 우편으로 부치렵니다.
5. I sop'orŭl paep'yŏnŭro puch'iryŏmnida.
   이 소포를 배편으로 부치렵니다.
6. Up'yorŭl ŏlmana puch'imyŏn toemnikka?
   우표를 얼마나 부치면 됩니까?
7. I p'yŏnjirŭl tŭnggi up'yŏnŭro puch'iryŏmnida.
   이 편지를 등기 우편으로 부치렵니다.
8. Ŏlmana ppalli paedaldoemnikka?
   얼마나 빨리 배달됩니까?
9. Kŏgie toch'ak'aryŏmyŏn ŏlmana kŏllimnikka?
   거기에 도착하려면 얼마나 걸립니까?
10. I yangshige ssŏ nŏŭshipshio.
    이 양식에 써 넣으십시오.

## 1. At the Information Desk of the Central Post Office

**Mr. Johnson** : Excuse me, where can I mail these letters to America?

**Information** : Turn to the right there (*pointing*) and walk down the corridor.

Then ask at the window No.3 on your right.

**Mr. Johnson** : Thank you.

* * *

**Mr. Johnson** : I'd like to mail these letters to America. How much will the postage be?

**Clerk** : Let me weigh your letters.

(*He weighs each letter.*)

440 won for these two letters, and 620 won this one.

## 1. 중앙 우체국의 안내대에서

J : Mianhamnidaman, Miguge ponaenŭn i p'yŏnji ŏdiesŏ puch'imnikka?
미안합니다만, 미국에 보내는 이 편지 어디에서 부칩니까?

I : Chŏgisŏ orŭnp'yŏnŭro torasŏ poktorŭl kŏrŏ naeryŏgashipshio. Kŭrigo orŭnp'yŏne sambŏn ch'angguesŏ murŏ poshipshio.
저기서(가리키면서) 오른편으로 돌아서 복도를 걸어 내려가십시오. 그리고 오른편에 삼번 창구에서 물어 보십시오.

J : Kamsahamnida.
감사합니다.

* * *

J : I p'yŏnji Miguge puch'iryŏmnida.
Up'yorŭl ŏlmana puch'imnikka?
이 편지 미국에 부치렵니다.
우표를 얼마나 부칩니까?

C : P'yŏnjirŭl tara pogessŭmnida.
편지를 달아 보겠습니다.

(그는 편지를 각각 단다.)

I p'yŏnjidŭrŭn sabaeksashibwŏnigo, igŏsŭn yukpaegishibwŏnimnida.
이 편지들은 사백사십원이고, 이것은 육백이십원입니다.

**Mr. Johnson :** Here's the money.

**Clerk :** Yes, sir.

## 2. Registered Mail

**Miss Smith :** I would like to send this letter to London by registered mail, please.

**Clerk :** By air, Miss?

**Miss Smith :** Yes, by air mail.

**Clerk :** One moment. Let's see. It weighs 352 grammes. That'll be 8,100 won plus 800 won for the registration. 8,900 won, please.

**Miss Smith :** Here's a 10,000 won bill.

**Clerk :** Here's your change and the receipt.

**Miss Smith :** Thank you. By the way, I need a dozen aerograms, please.

**Clerk :** Ask at window No.7, please.

**Miss Smith :** Thank you.

J : Yŏgi ton issŭmnida. 여기 돈 있습니다.
C : Ne. 네.

## 2. 등기 우편

S : I p'yŏnjirŭl tŭnggiro Rŏndŏnŭro ponaeryŏmnida.
이 편지를 등기로 런던으로 보내렵니다.
C : Hanggongimnikka?
항공입니까?
S : Ne, hanggong up'yŏnŭroyo.
네, 항공 우편으로요.
C : Chamkkanmanyo. Popshida. Mugega sambaegoshipi kŭraem nagamnida.
P'alch'ŏnbaegwŏne tŭnggiryo p'albaegwŏn, p'alch'ŏn-gubaegwŏni toemnida.
잠깐만요. 봅시다. 무게가 삼백오십이그램 나갑니다.
팔천백원에 등기료 팔백원, 팔천구백원이 됩니다.
S : Yŏgi manwŏntchari issŭmnida.
여기 만원짜리 있습니다.
C : Yŏgi kŏsŭrŭmton-gwa yŏngsujŭng issŭmnida.
여기 거스름돈과 영수증 있습니다.
S : Kamsahamnida. Ch'am, kŭrigo hanggong yŏpsŏ yŏltu chang saryŏmnida.
감사합니다. 참, 그리고 항공 엽서 열두 장 사렵니다.
C : Ch'ilbŏn ch'anggueső murŏ poshipshio.
칠번 창구에서 물어 보십시오.
S : Kamsahamnida.
감사합니다.

## 3. In Front of the Gate of the International Parcel Post Office

**Mrs. Green :** Where do I mail these parcels, please?

**Gate Guard :** Go up this way and turn to left. You'll find an entrance in the middle of the building.

**Mrs. Green :** Thank you.

**Gate Guard :** You're welcome.

## 4. At the Information Desk

**Mrs. Green :** I'd like to send these parcels to America.

**Information :** Go to that corner on your right, and get your customs clearance first. Then, ask the clerk at the counter.

**Mrs. Green :** Thank you.

## 3. 국제 소포 우체국 앞에서

Gr: I sop'orŭl ŏdiesŏ puch'imnikka?
이 소포를 어디에서 부칩니까?

G : I kirŭl ollagashidaga oenp'yŏnŭro toragashipshio. Kŏnmul chungange ipkuga issŭmnida.
이 길을 올라가시다가 왼편으로 돌아가십시오. 건물 중앙에 입구가 있습니다.

Gr: Kamsahamnida.
감사합니다.

G : Ch'ŏnmaneyo.
천만에요.

## 4. 안내대에서

G : I sop'orŭl Miguge puch'iryŏmnida.
이 소포를 미국에 부치렵니다.

I : Orŭnp'yŏn chŏ mot'ungiro kasyŏsŏ mŏnjŏ t'onggwan susogŭl hashipshio.
Kŭrigo k'aunt'ŏesŏ chigwŏnege murŭshipshio.
오른편 저 모퉁이로 가셔서 먼저 통관 수속을 하십시오.
그리고 카운터에서 직원에게 물으십시오.

G : Kamsahamnida.
감사합니다.

## 5. At the Customs Officer's Desk

**Officer :** What are these, Ma'am?

**Mrs. Green :** This parcel contains 500 grammes of ginseng and this one contain a dozen gift items.

**Officer :** What kind of gifts are they?

**Mrs. Green :** These are several Korean silk scarfs, a couple of folding fans, brass ashtrays and wooden carvings.
They are for my family back home.

**Officer :** All right. Fill in these forms, please.

**Mrs. Green :** Do I have to pay any tax?

**Officer :** No, I don't think so. You are allowed to send up to 700 grammes of ginseng, and there's no tax for the small gift items.

**Mrs. Green :** Thank you.

## 5. 세관원석에서

O : Igŏttŭri muŏshimnikka, puin?
이것들이 무엇입니까, 부인?

G : I sop'oenŭn insami obaek kŭraem tŭrŏ itko, yŏgienŭn sŏnmuri han yŏltu kae tŭrŏ issŭmnida.
이 소포에는 인삼이 오백 그램 들어 있고, 여기에는 선물이 한 열두 개 들어 있습니다.

O : Musŭn chongnyuŭi sŏnmurimnikka?
무슨 종류의 선물입니까?

G : Han-guk myŏngju sŭk'ap'ŭ myŏt chang, chŏmnŭn puch'ae tu kae, yugi chaettŏriwa mokkaktŭrimnida. Igŏttŭrŭn chibe innŭn kajogege ponaenŭn kŏshimnida.
한국 명주 스카프 몇 장, 접는 부채 두 개, 유기 재떨이와 목각들입니다. 이것들은 집에 있는 가족에게 보내는 것입니다.

O : Arassŭmnida. I chongie ssŏ nŏŭshipshio.
알았읍니다. 이 종이에 써 넣으십시오.

G : Segŭmŭl murŏya toemnikka?
세금을 물어야 됩니까?

O : Anio, an naedo toel kŏmnida. Insamŭn ch'ilbaek kŭraemkkaji ponael su itko, chagŭn sŏnmurenŭn segŭmi ŏpsŭmnida.
아니오, 안 내도 될 겁니다. 인삼은 칠백 그램까지 보낼 수 있고, 작은 선물에는 세금이 없습니다.

G : Kamsahamnida. 감사합니다.

## 6. At the Counter

**Mrs. Green :** I want to send these two packages by sea mail, please.

**Clerk :** Yes, Ma'am.

(*He weighs the parcels.*)

2,400 won for this one and 4,500 won for this, Ma'am.

**Mrs. Green :** All right. How long will it take for them to get to America?

**Clerk :** Oh, about five to six weeks, at the most.

**Mrs. Green :** I see. Well, there's no hurry. Here's the money.

**Clerk :** Thank you. Here's your receipt, Ma'am. Good-bye.

**Mrs. Green :** Thank you. Good-bye.

## 6. 카운터에서

G : I sop'orŭl paep'yŏnŭro puch'iryŏmnida.
이 소포를 배편으로 부치렵니다.

C : Ne, puin.
네, 부인.

(그는 소포 무게를 단다.)
Igŏsŭn ich'ŏnsabaegwŏnigo, igŏsŭn sach'ŏnobaegwŏnimnida, puin.
이것은 이천사백원이고, 이것은 사천오백원입니다, 부인.

G : Arassŭmnida.
Miguge toch'aktoeryŏmyŏn ŏlmana kŏllimnikka?
알았습니다.
미국에 도착되려면 얼마나 걸립니까?

C : Ne, taegae ojuesŏ yukchutchŭm kŏllimnida.
네, 대개 오주에서 육주쯤 걸립니다.

G : Kŭraeyo. Kŭp'ajinŭn anssŭmnida. Yŏgi ton issŭmnida.
그래요. 급하지는 않습니다. 여기 돈 있습니다.

C : Kamsahamnida. Yŏngsujŭng padŭseyo, puin.
Annyŏnghi kashipshio.
감사합니다. 영수증 받으세요, 부인.
안녕히 가십시오.

G : Kamsahamnida.
Annyŏnghi kyeshipshio.
감사합니다.
안녕히 계십시오.

## 7. Sending a Telegram

(*At the information desk*)

**Mr. Hoover :** Where can I send a cable?

**Information :** Go up to the second floor and go into the room to your right.

**Mr. Hoover :** Thank you.

* * *

**Mr. Hoover :** Please give me a telegram form.

**Clerk :** They are on the writing desk over there, sir.

**Mr. Hoover :** Thank you. By the way, can I use a typewriter?

**Clerk :** Yes. Please come around that way. You can use one of these.

(*Finishes typing*)

**Mr. Hoover :** Here it is.

What is the rate?

## 7. 전보치기

(안내대에서)

**H** : Ŏdisŏ kukche chŏnborŭl ch'il su issŭmnikka?
어디서 국제 전보를 칠 수 있습니까?

**I** : Ich'ŭngŭro ollagasŏ orŭnp'yŏn pangŭro tŭrŏgashipshio.
이층으로 올라가서 오른편 방으로 들어가십시오.

**H** : Kamsahamnida.
감사합니다.

* * *

**H** : Chŏnbo yongjirŭl chushipshio.
전보 용지를 주십시오.

**C** : Chŏgi ch'aeksang wie issŭmnida.
저기 책상 위에 있습니다.

**H** : Kamsahamnida. Kŭrŏnde t'aip'ŭrŭl ssŭl su issŭmnikka?
감사합니다. 그런데 타이프를 쓸 수 있습니까?

**C** : Ne, chŏriro torasŏ oshipshio. I chungesŏ ŏnŭ kŏna ssŭseyo.
네, 저리로 돌아서 오십시오. 이 중에서 어느 거나 쓰세요.

(타이프를 끝내고)

**H** : Yŏgi issŭmnida. Ŏlmajyo?
여기 있습니다. 얼마죠?

**Clerk :** It is 3,850 won for up to 22 words and every additional word costs 175 won each.

(*The clerk reads the form and looks at the table.*) It'll be 7,000 won, sir.

**Mr. Hoover :** Here's a 10, 000 won bill.

**Clerk :** Thank you. Here's your change and the receipt.

Post Office

C : Ishibi tanŏkkaji samch'ŏnp'albaegoshibwŏnigo,han tanŏ ch'ugahal ttaemada paekch'ilshibowŏnŭl tŏhamnida.
이십이단어까지 삼천팔백오십원이고, 한 단어 추가할 때마다 백칠십오원을 더합니다.
(직원은 전보 용지를 읽고 계산표를 본다.)
Ch'ilch'ŏnwŏni toegessŭmnida.
칠천원이 되겠습니다.

H : Manwŏntcharimnida.
만원짜립니다.

C : Kamsahamnida.
Kŏsŭrŭmton-gwa yŏngsujŭng padŭseyo.
감사합니다. 거스름돈과 영수증 받으세요.

Public Telephone

# VIII. AT THE BARBER'S

## ☐ Useful Expressions

1. Where is the nearest barber shop?
2. How much do you charge for a haircut?
3. I just need a shave.
4. Don't shave too close, please.
5. I want only a shampoo.
6. Leave my sideburns as they are.
7. Please trim the moustache neatly.
8. I don't need a manicure.
9. Apply just a little bit of hair oil.
10. I'm in a hurry. Don't take too long, please.

# VIII. 이발소에서

## □ 많이 쓰는 표현

1. Cheil kakkaun ibalsoga ŏdi issŭmnikka?
   제일 가까운 이발소가 어디 있습니까?
2. Iballyonŭn ŏlmaimnikka?
   이발료는 얼마입니까?
3. Myŏndoman hagessŭmnida.
   면도만 하겠습니다.
4. Nŏmu p'aji maseyo.
   너무 파지 마세요.
5. Mŏriman kama chuseyo.
   머리만 감아 주세요.
6. Kurenarusŭn kŭnyang tuseyo.
   구레나룻은 그냥 두세요.
7. K'ossuyŏmŭn chal tadŭmŏ chuseyo.
   콧수염은 잘 다듬어 주세요.
8. Sont'op sonjirŭn p'iryoŏpsŭmnida.
   손톱 손질은 필요 없습니다.
9. Kirŭmŭn chogŭmman palla chuseyo.
   기름은 조금만 발라 주세요.
10. Pappŭmnida.
    Nŏmu orae haji maseyo.
    바쁩니다.
    너무 오래 하지 마세요.

## At the Barber's

**Receptionist :** Good afternoon. Would you like a haircut, sir?

**Mr. Hoover :** Yes, please.

**Receptionist :** This way, please. Would you like to change your shoes into slippers?

**Mr. Hoover :** Fine, that would be comfortable.

**Receptionist :** Let me have your coat, please.

(*She receives his coat.*)

Please take a seat over here.

* * *

**Barber :** Good afternoon. How would you like your haircut?

**Mr. Hoover :** Just trim a little on the sides, and clip off the long hair on the top.

## 이발소에서

R : Ŏsŏ oshipshio.
Ibarhashiryŏmnikka?
어서 오십시오.
이발하시렵니까?

H : Ne.
네.

R : Iriro oshipshio. Sŭllip'ŏro pakkwŏ shinŭshipshio.
이리로 오십시오.
슬리퍼로 바꿔 신으십시오.

H : Chossŭmnida. P'yŏnanhagetkunyo.
좋습니다. 편안하겠군요.

R : Utchŏgorirŭl chushipshio.
웃저고리를 주십시오.
(그녀는 웃저고리를 받는다.)
Chŏgi chŏ charie anjŭshipshio.
저기 저 자리에 앉으십시오.

*　　*　　*

B : Annyŏnghashimnikka? Ŏttŏk'e kkakkŭshilkkayo?
안녕하십니까?
어떻게 깎으실까요?

H : Yangp'yŏnŭl chom kkakko, wie innŭn kin mŏrirŭl charŭshipshio. Twinmŏrinŭn kilji anch'iyo? Kŭrŏch'yo?

The hair in the back isn't too long, is it?

**Barber :** No, it's not. Just about right, sir.

(*He finishes the trimming.*)

Now, how do you like it, sir?

**Mr. Hoover :** That's a good job!

**Barber :** Do you want a shave, sir?

**Mr. Hoover :** Yes, please, but not too close.

**Barber :** I understand, sir.

(*Finishes shaving.*)

**Barber :** Would you like a shampoo, sir?

**Mr. Hoover :** Yes, please. Don't scrub the hair too hard.

(*Finishes the shampoo.*)

**Barber :** You would like a massage on the shoulder, if you are not in a hurry.

**Mr. Hoover :** No, I'm not in a hurry.

양편을 좀 깎고 위에 있는 긴 머리를 자르십시오. 뒷머리는 길지 않지요? 그렇죠?

B : Ne, kilji anayo.
Kkok chossŭmnida.
네, 길지 않아요.
꼭 좋습니다.

(그는 깎기를 끝낸다.)
Cha, ŏttŏssŭmnikka?
자, 어떻습니까?

H : Chal toeŏssŭmnida.
잘 되었습니다.

B : Myŏndohashiryŏmnikka?
면도하시렵니까?

H : Ne, kŭrŏna nŏmu p'aji mashipshio.
네, 그러나 너무 파지 마십시오.

B : Arassŭmnida.
알았습니다.

(면도를 끝낸다.)

B : Syamp'uhalkkayo?
샴푸할까요?

H : Ne, nŏmu mŏrirŭl kŭkchi maseyo.
네, 너무 머리를 긁지 마세요.

(샴푸를 끝낸다.)

B : Pappŭji anŭshimyŏn ŏkkaerŭl chumullŏ tŭrilkkayo?
바쁘지 않으시면 어깨를 주물러 드릴까요?

H : Pappŭji anayo. Chogŭmman hae chusyŏssŭmyŏn chok'essŏyo. Kibun chossŭmnida.

I would appreciate a little. That feels wonderful.

(*As he gets up from the chair.*)

How much do I owe you?

**Receptionist :** That'll be 12,000 won including everything.

**Mr. Hoover :** Here's the money.

That was an excellent haircut.

**Receptionist :** Good-bye. Please come back again.

**Mr. Hoover :** Good-bye.

Barbershop

바쁘지 않아요. 조금만 해 주셨으면 좋겠어요. 기분 좋습니다.

(의자에서 일어나며)

Ŏlmaimnikka?

얼마입니까?

**R** : Modu hap'aesŏ manich'ŏnwŏni toegessŭmnida.

모두 합해서 만이천원이 되겠습니다.

**H** : Ton padŭseyo.

Ibal chal hayŏssŭmnida.

돈 받으세요.

이발 잘 하였습니다.

**R** : Annyŏnghi kashipshio. Tto oshipshio.

안녕히 가십시오. 또 오십시오.

**H** : Annyŏnghi kyeshipshio.

안녕히 계십시오.

# IX. AT THE PHOTO SHOP

## ☐ Useful Expressions

1. Please give me a roll of color film.
2. What brand of color film do you have?
3. Do you want color slidefilms or negatives for prints?
4. I want a roll of black and white film.
5. Do you have 36 exposures?
6. I want these films developed.
7. What is the standard size?
8. Can you enlarge these to 5″ × 7″?
9. How long will it take to be ready?
10. Can you mail the developed slides to my address?

# IX. 사진 재료상에서

## □ 많이 쓰는 표현

1. K'ŏllŏ p'illŭm han t'ong chuseyo.
   컬러 필름 한 통 주세요.
2. Ŏttŏn chongnyuŭi k'ŏllŏ p'illŭmi issŭmnikka?
   어떤 종류의 컬러 필름이 있습니까?
3. K'ŏllŏ sŭllaidŭ p'illŭmŭl wŏnhashimnikka, ttonŭn negarŭl wŏnhashimnikka?
   컬러 슬라이드 필름을 원하십니까, 또는 네가를 원하십니까?
4. Hŭkpaek p'illŭm han t'ong chushipshio.
   흑백 필름 한 통 주십시오.
5. Sŏrŭnyŏsŏt changtchari issŭmnikka?
   서른여섯 장짜리 있습니까?
6. I p'illŭmŭl hyŏnsanghae chuseyo.
   이 필름을 현상해 주세요.
7. P'yojunhyŏngŭn ŏttŏn k'ŭgiimnikka?
   표준형은 어떤 크기입니까?
8. O inch'i ch'il inch'iro hwaktaehal su issŭmnikka?
   오 인치 칠 인치로 확대할 수 있습니까?
9. Ta toeryŏmyŏn ŏlmana kŏllimnikka?
   다 되려면 얼마나 걸립니까?
10. Hyŏnsanghan sŭllaidŭrŭl che chusoro ponae chul su issŭmnikka?
    현상한 슬라이드를 제 주소로 보내 줄 수 있습니까?

## At the Photo Shop

**Miss Jade :** I'd like to leave this roll of film to be developed.

**Clerk :** Yes, Miss. And would you like to have a print of each frame at the same time?

**Miss Jade :** Yes, please. What size do you have?

**Clerk :** The standard size is 3″ × 4″ shown here in the middle.

**Miss Jade :** What is the price?

**Clerk :** 220 won each. It's a good bargain and service is fast.

**Miss Jade :** When will they be ready?

**Clerk :** You can come back any time after Wednesday.

## 사진 재료상에서

J : I p'illŭmŭi hyŏnsangŭl matkiryŏmnida.
이 필름의 현상을 맡기렵니다.

C : Ne, agassi.
Kŭrigo inhwado hanassik hamkke hashiryŏmnikka?
네, 아가씨.
그리고 인화도 하나씩 함께 하시렵니까?

J : Ne, kŭrŏk'e hae chuseyo.
Ŏttŏn saijŭga itchyo?
네, 그렇게 해 주세요.
어떤 사이즈가 있죠?

C : P'yojun saijŭnŭn yŏgi kaunde innŭn sam inch'i sa inch'iimnida.
표준 사이즈는 여기 가운데 있는 삼 인치, 사 인치입니다.

J : Kapshi ŏlmajyo?
값이 얼마죠?

C : Han change ibaegishibwŏnimnida. Ssago sŏbisŭdo pparŭdamnida.
한 장에 이백이십원입니다.
싸고 서비스도 빠르답니다.

J : Ŏnje toemnikka?
언제 됩니까?

C : Suyoil ihubut'ŏnŭn ŏnjedŭnji oseyo.
수요일 이후부터는 언제든지 오세요.

**Miss Jade :** All right. And I need another roll of color negative film, please.

**Clerk :** What brand do you prefer? We have Kodachrome, Ektachrome and Agfa.

**Miss Jade :** I prefer Ektachrome.

**Clerk :** Here it is. 20 exposures.

**Miss Jade :** Don't you have 36 exposures?

**Clerk :** No, we are out of them.

**Miss Jade :** Then, I would like another roll, please. How much is it a roll?

**Clerk :** A 20 exposures roll is 4,800 won.

**Miss Jade :** Here's 5,000 won bill.

**Clerk :** Thank you. Here's your change. Good-bye.

**Miss Jade :** Good-bye.

J : Arassŭmnida. Kŭrigo k'ŏllŏ nega p'illŭmŭl han t'ong saryŏmnida.
알았습니다. 그리고 컬러 네가 필름을 한 통 사렵니다.

C : Ŏttŏn sangp'yorŭl choahaseyo? K'odak'ŭrom, ek-t'ak'ŭromgwa agŭp'aga issŭmnida.
어떤 상표를 좋아하세요? 코다크롬, 엑타크롬과 아그파가 있습니다.

J : Ekt'ak'ŭromi tŏ maŭme tŭrŏyo.
엑타크롬이 더 마음에 들어요.

C : Yŏgi issŭmnida. Sŭmu changtchariimnida.
여기 있습니다. 스무 장짜리입니다.

J : Sŏrŭnyŏsŏt changtcharinŭn ŏpsŭmnikka?
서른여섯 장짜리는 없습니까?

C : Ne, ta nagassŭmnida.
네, 다 나갔습니다.

J : Kŭrŏm hana tŏ chushipshio. Han t'onge ŏlmaimnikka?
그럼 하나 더 주십시오. 한 통에 얼마입니까?

C : Sŭmu changtcharinŭn sach'ŏnp'albaegwŏnimnida.
스무 장짜리는 사천팔백원입니다.

J : Yŏgi och'ŏnwŏntchari issŭmnida.
여기 오천원짜리 있습니다.

C : Kamsahamnida. Kŏsŭrŭmton padŭseyo. Annyŏnghi kashipshio.
감사합니다. 거스름돈 받으세요. 안녕히 가십시오.

J : Annyŏnghi kyeshipshio.
안녕히 계십시오.

# X. AT THE TAILOR'S

## □ Useful Expressions

1. I need a suite.
   Where do you suggest?
2. Do you want one made to an order?
3. I want a ready-made one.
4. Tailor-mades are not too expensive in Korea.
5. Do you know of any good tailor's?
6. Let's try one near Chosun Hotel.
7. This material is 70% polyester and 30% wool.
8. When shall I come back for a fitting?
9. Make it a little loose.

# X. 양복점에서

## □ 많이 쓰는 표현

1. Yangbogi han pŏl p'iryohamnida. Ŏdiro ka polkkayo?
   양복이 한 벌 필요합니다.
   어디로 가 볼까요?
2. Mach'umosŭl wŏnhashimnikka?
   맞춤옷을 원하십니까?
3. Kisŏngbogŭl wŏnhamnida.
   기성복을 원합니다.
4. Han-gugesŏnŭn mach'umoshi kŭri pissaji anssŭmnida.
   한국에서는 맞춤옷이 그리 비싸지 않습니다.
5. Choŭn yangbokchŏmŭl ashimnikka?
   좋은 양복점을 아십니까?
6. Chosŏn hot'el kŭnch'ŏe ka popshida.
   조선 호텔 근처에 가 봅시다.
7. I kamŭn ch'ilship p'ŏsent'ŭ p'olliesŭt'erŭwa samship p'ŏsent'ŭ moimnida.
   이 감은 칠십 퍼센트 폴리에스테르와 삼십 퍼센트 모입니다.
8. Kabongharŏ ŏnje olkkayo?
   가봉하러 언제 올까요?
9. Chom nŏngnŏk'i hae chuseyo.
   좀 넉넉히 해 주세요.

10. I think it's a little too tight.

## At the Tailor's

**Clerk :** Good afternoon, sir.

**Mr. Dubois :** Good afternoon.

**Clerk :** Would you like a suit madé to an order?

**Mr. Dubois :** Yes, I'd like one in a hurry. How soon can you finish one?

**Clerk :** We can deliver in 3 days. Will that be soon enough?

**Mr. Dubois :** Yes, I think so.

**Clerk :** All right, would you choose the material you'd like, please.

**Mr. Dubois :** I think this looks good.

**Clerk :** Yes, that's the latest and it's 100% wool, sir.

A suit from that will be 350,000 won.

10. Chom kkinŭn kŏt kassŭmnida.
좀 끼는 것 같습니다.

## 양복점에서

C : Ŏsŏ oshipshio.
어서 오십시오.

D : Annyŏnghashimnikka?
안녕하십니까?

C : Yangbok mach'ushiryŏmnikka?
양복 맞추시렵니까?

D : Ne, kŭp'i hago ship'ŭndeyo. Ŏlmana ppalli hal su issŭlkkayo?
네, 급히 하고 싶은데요. 얼마나 빨리 할 수 있을까요?

C : Samirimyŏn hae tŭril su issŭmnida. Kŭmanhamyŏn, toegessŭmnikka?
삼일이면 해 드릴 수 있습니다. 그만하면 되겠습니까?

D : Ne, chossŭmnida.
네, 좋습니다.

C : Ne, kŭrŏm mame tŭshinŭn kamŭl korŭshipshio.
네, 그럼 맘에 드시는 감을 고르십시오.

D : Igŏshi choŭl kŏt kassŭmnida.
이것이 좋을 것 같습니다.

C : Ne, kŭgŏsŭn ch'oeshinŭi kŏshigo paek p'ŏsent'ŭ mojigimnida. Igŏsŭro yangbok han pŏre samsip-omanwŏni toegessŭmnida.
네, 그것은 최신의 것이고 백 퍼센트 모직입니다. 이것으로 양복 한 벌에 삼십오만원이 되겠습니다.

**Mr. Dubois :** That's fine.

**Clerk :** Will you come this way for measuring?

Please take off your coat.

**Mr. Dubois :** O.K. I'd like a three button coat as illustrated in that picture.

**Clerk :** Yes, sir.

(*After a while*)

**Clerk :** Please drop in tomorrow morning for a fitting.

**Mr. Dubois :** O.K. I'll be along around noon.

**Clerk :** Thank you. Good-bye, sir.

Tailor Shop

D : Chossŭmnida.
좋습니다.

C : Ch'isurŭl chaege iriro oshilkkayo? Utchŏgorirŭl pŏsŭshijiyo.
치수를 재게 이리로 오실까요? 웃저고리를 벗으시지요.

D : Ne, chŏ kŭrime innŭn taero tanch'u se kaerŭl tara chuseyo.
네, 저 그림에 있는 대로 단추 세 개를 달아 주세요.

C : Arassŭmnida.
알았습니다.

(잠시 후)

C : Kabongŭl hashirŏ naeil ach'ime chom tŭllŭshijiyo.
가봉을 하시러 내일 아침에 좀 들르시지요.

D : Ne, chŏmshimttaetchŭm tŭllŭgessŭmnida.
네, 점심때쯤 들르겠습니다.

C : Kamsahamnida. Annyŏnghi kashipshio.
감사합니다. 안녕히 가십시오.

Dressmaking Shop

# XI. FINDING A RENT HOUSE

## □ Useful Expressions

1. I want to rent a small room.
2. The room has a small kitchenette and a bath.
3. What does a *kong-in chunggaesa* do?
4. It's a kind of real estate agent.
5. How do I pay for the rent?
6. You should provide the guaranty money first.
7. Monthly rent is 350,000 won.
8. What does *chonseton* mean?
9. You pay rather a large sum for the room, and will get your entire money back when you leave.

# XI. 셋집을 찾아서

## □ 많이 쓰는 표현

1. Chagŭn pang serŭl tŭlgo shipsŭmnida.
   작은 방 세를 들고 싶습니다.
2. Kŭ pangenŭn chagŭn chubanggwa mogyokshiri issŭmnida.
   그 방에는 작은 주방과 목욕실이 있습니다.
3. Kong-in Chunggaesanŭn ŏttŏn irŭl hamnikka?
   공인중개사는 어떤 일을 합니까?
4. Pudongsan sogaeŏbŭi han chongnyuimnida.
   부동산 소개업의 한 종류입니다.
5. Serŭl ŏttŏk'e naejiyo?
   세를 어떻게 내지요?
6. Mŏnjŏ pojŭnggŭmŭl maryŏnhaeya hamnida.
   먼저 보증금을 마련해야 합니다.
7. Wŏlsenŭn shibomanwŏnimnida.
   월세는 십오만원입니다.
8. Chŏnsetoniran musŭn ttŭshimnikka?
   전세돈이란 무슨 뜻입니까?
9. Setpang ŏdŭl ttae chom k'ŭndonŭl naeshigo, ttŏnashil ttae tonŭl ta tollyŏ padŭshinŭn kŏmnida.
   셋방 얻을 때 좀 큰돈을 내시고, 떠나실 때 돈을 다 돌려 받으시는 겁니다.

10. There is no monthly rent to pay.

## 1. Finding a Rent House

**Agent :** Good morning. May I help you?

**Mr. Smith :** I am trying to find a room for myself.

**Agent :** I have just the room to offer you.

It's a western style room with bath and small kitchenette.

**Mr. Smith :** Who is the owner?

**Agent :** The proprietor is a small businessman. He is looking for a single man.

**Mr. Smith :** What is the rent?

**Agent :** It is 150,000 won a month. But you must pay six months rent in advance.

**Mr. Smith :** Oh, boy. That's not easy.

**Agent :** But, sir. It's really an ideal place.

10. Wŏlsenŭn **naeji** anado toemnida.
월세는 내지 않아도 됩니다.

## 1. 셋집을 찾아서

A : Ŏsŏ oshipshio. Muŏsŭl ch'ajŭshimnikka?
어서 오십시오. 무엇을 찾으십니까?

S : Pangŭl hana **kuhar**yŏmnida.
방을 하나 **구하렵니다**.

A : **Paro sogaehal man**han pangi issŭmnida. **Yokshilgwa** chagŭn chubang shisŏrŭl katch'un sŏyangshik pangimnida.
바로 소개할 만한 방이 있습니다. 욕실과 작은 주방 시설을 갖춘 서양식 방입니다.

S : Chuinŭn nugushijyo? 주인은 누구시죠?

A : Chipchuinŭn sogyumoŭi saŏpkaimnida. Kŭnŭn namja honjain punŭl ch'atko issŭmnida.
집주인은 소규모의 사업가입니다. 그는 남자 혼자인 분을 찾고 있습니다.

S : Settonŭn ŏlmaimnikka? 셋돈은 얼마입니까?

A : Han tare shibomanwŏnimnida. Kŭrigo yuk kaewŏlbunŭl miri naesyŏya hamnida.
한 달에 십오만원입니다. 그리고 육 개월분을 미리 내셔야 합니다.

S : Aigu ch'am, kŭgŏsŭn ŏryŏundeyo.
아이구 참, 그것은 어려운데요.

A : Kŭrŏna sŏnsaengnim, chŏngmal pangi chossŭmnida. 그러나 선생님, 정말 방이 좋습니다.

**Mr. Smith :** How far is it?

**Agent :** It's only a three minute walk from here. If you're interested in it, we could go and see it right now.

**Mr. Smith :** O.K. Let's.

## 2. Inspecting a House to Rent

**Agent :** Come this way, Mr. & Mrs. Thomson.

This is the entrance and there are two big rooms on both sides.

**Mr. Thomson :** Good. Where's the garage?

**Agent :** It's around the left of the house.

**Mrs. Thomson :** The outside looks all right to me.

Can we see the inside now?

**Agent :** Of course, Ma'am.
This way, please.

S : Ŏlmana mŏmnikka?
얼마나 멉니까?

A : Yŏgisŏ kŏrŏsŏ sambunbakke an kŏllimnida. Pangŭl poshiryŏmyŏn chigŭm kot kasŏ pol su issŭmnida.
여기서 걸어서 삼분밖에 안 걸립니다. 방을 보시려면 지금 곧 가서 볼 수 있습니다.

S : Chossŭmnida. Ka popshida.
좋습니다. 가 봅시다.

## 2. 셋집을 돌아보면서

A : Iriro oshipshio.
Yŏgiga ipkuigo, yangtchogŭro k'ŭn pang tu kaega issŭmnida.
이리로 오십시오.
여기가 입구이고 양쪽으로 큰 방 두 개가 있습니다.

Mr: Chok'unyo.
Ch'agoga ŏdi issŭmnikka?
좋군요.
차고가 어디 있습니까?

A : Chip oentchogŭro toragamyŏn issŭmnida.
집 왼쪽으로 돌아가면 있습니다.

Ms.: Oegwanŭn chok'unyo. Kŭrŏm chibanŭl pol su issŭlkkayo?
외관은 좋군요. 그럼 집안을 볼 수 있을까요?

A : Mullonimnida, puin. Itchogŭro oshipshio.
물론입니다, 부인. 이쪽으로 오십시오.

* * *

**Mrs. Thomson :** The rooms are quite agreeable.

Is that the way to the kitchen?

**Mr. Thomson :** Wait a little, dear, while I look into the study.

**Agent :** Yes, that's the way to the dining room and the kitchen, Ma'am.

And the bathroom is over here.

**Mr. Thomson :** The study is quite bright. Now, let's go into the dining room and the kitchen.

* * *

**Mr. Thomson :** The kitchen is spacious, too. Now shall we look into the bathroom?

*　　*　　*

**Ms.:** Pangdŭri aju maŭme tŭmnida. Chŏtchogŭro puŏk'e kanŭn-gayo?
방들이 아주 마음에 듭니다. 저쪽으로 부엌에 가는가요?

**Mr.:** Sŏjaerŭl tŭryŏdaboge chamkkanman kidaryŏyo, yŏbo.
서재를 들여다보게 잠깐만 기다려요, 여보.

**A :** Ne, chŏtchogŭro shiktanggwa puŏk'ŭro tŭrŏgamnida, puin.
Kŭrigo yokshirŭn yŏgie issŭmnida.
네, 저쪽으로 식당과 부엌으로 들어갑니다, 부인.
그리고 욕실은 여기에 있습니다.

**Mr.:** Sŏjaega aju paksŭmnida.
Cha, kŭrŏm shiktanggwa puŏk'ŭro tŭrŏga popshida.
서재가 아주 밝습니다.
자, 그럼 식당과 부엌으로 들어가 봅시다.

*　　*　　*

**Mr.:** Puŏkto nŏlssŭmnida. Kŭrŏm yokshil chom polkkayo?
부엌도 넓습니다.
그럼 욕실 좀 볼까요?

**Mrs. Thomson :** I like the house, dear. What do you think?

**Mr. Thomson :** So do I. I'll come by tomorrow afternoon to finalize the contract.

**Agent :** All right, sir. I'll be waiting for you at my office. Good-bye.

**Ms.:** Yŏbo, na i chibi maŭme tŭrŏyo. Ŏttŏk'e saeng-gak'aseyo?
여보, 나 이 집이 마음에 들어요. 어떻게 생각하세요?

**Mr.:** Nado kŭraeyo. Naeil ohue kyeyak'arŏ ogessŏyo.
나도 그래요. 내일 오후에 계약하러 오겠어요.

**A :** Chossŭmnida. Che samushiresŏ kidarigessŭmnida. Annyŏnghi kashipshio.
좋습니다. 제 사무실에서 기다리겠습니다. 안녕히 가십시오.

Real Estate Agency

# XII. SIGHTSEEING

## □ Useful Expressions

1. How long will you stay in Seoul?
2. I will stay about one month.
3. When will you leave for Gyeongju?
4. I will leave for Cheju-do tomorrow.
5. Where's the express bus terminal?
   Where's the taxi stand?
6. Please tell me how to get to the Chosun Hotel.
7. How far is Pusan from here?
8. It's about 20 miles from here.
9. How long does it take to get there?
10. It usually takes about one hour.

# XII. 관 광

## □ 많이 쓰는 표현

1. Ŏlma tongan Sŏure mŏmurŭshigessŭmnikka?
   얼마 동안 서울에 머무르시겠습니까?
2. Yak han tal mŏmurŭgessŭmnida.
   약 한 달 머무르겠습니다.
3. Ŏnje Kyŏngjuro ttŏnashigessŭmnikka?
   언제 경주로 떠나시겠습니까?
4. Naeil Chejudoro ttŏnagessŭmnida.
   내일 제주도로 떠나겠습니다.
5. Kosokpŏsŭ chŏngnyujangi ŏdie issŭmnikka?
   T'aekshi chŏngnyujangi ŏdi issŭmnikka?
   고속버스 정류장이 어디에 있습니까?
   택시 정류장이 어디 있습니까?
6. Chosŏn hot'ere karyŏmyŏn ŏttŏk'e kamnikka?
   조선 호텔에 가려면 어떻게 갑니까?
7. Yŏgisŏ Pusankkaji ŏlmana mŏmnikka?
   여기서 부산까지 얼마나 멉니까?
8. Yŏgisŏ yak iship mail toemnida.
   여기서 약 이십 마일 됩니다.
9. Kŏgie toch'ak'aryŏmyŏn ŏlmana kŏllimnikka?
   거기에 도착하려면 얼마나 걸립니까?
10. Pot'ong yak han shigan kŏllimnida.
    보통 약 한 시간 걸립니다.

11. Does this bus stop in front of City Hall?

12. Please let me off the bus at Chongno. (Please let me know when we get to Chongno.)

13. Do you know where this address is?

14. Could you draw me a map?

15. Is this the right way to the Chosun Hotel?

16. It is a little too far to walk.

17. How much is the night tour of the city?

18. How long does the tour take?

19. I would like to reserve two seats for the Kanghwa-do tour.

20. Your bus leaves at 10 in the morning.

### 1. In the Tearoom

**Mr. Williams :** Good afternoon, Mr. Lee.

**Mr. Lee :** Good afternoon, Mr. Williams.

11. I pŏsŭga shich'ŏng ap'e sŏmnikka?
이 버스가 시청 앞에 섭니까?
12. Chongno-esŏ naeryŏ chuseyo. (Chongno-e taŭ-myŏn allyŏ chuseyo.)
종로에서 내려 주세요. (종로에 닿으면 알려 주세요.)
13. I chusoga ŏdiinji ashimnikka?
이 주소가 어디인지 아십니까?
14. Chidorŭl kŭryŏ chushigessŭmnikka?
지도를 그려 주시겠습니까?
15. I kiri Chosŏn hot'ello kanŭn kirimnikka?
이 길이 조선 호텔로 가는 길입니까?
16. Kŏtkienŭn chom mŏmnida.
걷기에는 좀 멉니다.
17. Shinaeŭi yagan kwan-gwangŭn ŏlmaimnikka?
시내의 야간 관광은 얼마입니까?
18. Kugyŏnghanŭn te shigani ŏlmana kŏllimnikka?
구경하는 데 시간이 얼마나 걸립니까?
19. Kanghwado kwan-gwange tu chari yeyak'aryŏm-nida. 강화도 관광에 두 자리 예약하렵니다.
20. T'ashil pŏsŭga ach'im yŏlshie ch'ulbarhamnida.
타실 버스가 아침 열시에 출발합니다.

## 1. 다방에서

W : Annyŏnghashimnikka, I sŏnsaengnim.
안녕하십니까, 이 선생님.

L : Annyŏnghaseyo, Williŏmjŭ ssi. Ŏttŏk'e chinaese-yo?

How are you?

**Mr. Williams :** Fine. It's good to see you again. Let's sit down over there.

**Mr. Lee :** Yes. It's a beautiful day, isn't it?

**Mr. Williams :** Yes, it's a wonderful day for sightseeing.

**Mr. Lee :** Well, I am going to show you Kyongbok Palace first.

**Hostess :** What shall I serve you, sir?

**Mr. Lee :** What would you like, Mr. Williams? Coffee, tea, or Korean ginseng tea?

**Mr. Williams :** Coffee, please.

**Mr. Lee :** Two coffees, please.

**Hostess :** Yes, sir.

**Mr. Lee :** Well, as I was saying, I will show you the palace and the National Museum, first.

안녕하세요, 윌리엄즈 씨. 어떻게 지내세요?

W : Chossŭmnida. Tashi poepke toeŏ pan-gapsŭmnida. Chŏgi anjŭpshida.

좋습니다. 다시 뵙게 되어 반갑습니다. 저기 앉읍시다.

L : Ne. Nalssiga chossŭmnida, kŭrŏch'yo?

네, 날씨가 좋습니다. 그렇죠?

W : Ne, kwan-gwangenŭn hullyunghan narimnida.

네, 관광에는 훌륭한 날입니다.

L : Cha, mŏnjŏ Kyŏngbokkungŭl poyŏ tŭrigessŭmnida.

자, 먼저 경복궁을 보여 드리겠습니다.

H : Muŏsŭl tŭrilkkayo?

무엇을 드릴까요?

L : Muŏsŭl choahashimnikka, Williŏmjŭ ssi? k'ŏp'i hongch'a animyŏn Han-guk insamch'a tŭshigessŏyo?

무엇을 좋아하십니까, 윌리엄즈 씨? 커피, 홍차 아니면 한국 인삼차 드시겠어요?

W : K'ŏp'i hajiyo

커피 하지요.

L : K'ŏp'i tu chan chuseyo.

커피 두 잔 주세요.

H : Ne, arassŭmnida.

네, 알았습니다.

L : Ije malssŭmdŭrin taero mŏnjŏ kunggwa kungnip pangmulgwanbut'ŏ poyŏ tŭrigessŭmnida.

이제 말씀드린 대로 먼저 궁과 국립 박물관부터 보여 드리겠습니다.

**Mr. Williams :** That sounds good.

**Mr. Lee :** Then...

## 2. In the Palace

**Mr. Williams :** The lines of the roofs look elegant. I like them very much.

They are really unique.

**Mr. Lee :** Let's walk over there.

**Mr. Williams :** What is that building?

**Mr. Lee :** That's Kyonghoeru. Kings used to host many important celebrations or receive foreign guests there.

**Mr. Williams :** It certainly looks massive and beautiful.

**Mr. Lee :** Shall we take a little rest on the bench by the pond?

**Mr. Williams :** Yes, and I want to take some pictures, too.

W : Chossŭmnida.
좋습니다.

L : Kŭrŏm···
그럼···

## 2. 고궁에서

W : Chibungŭi sŏni uahamnida. Aju maŭme tŭmnida. Chŏngmal t'ŭgihagunyo.
지붕의 선이 우아합니다. 아주 마음에 듭니다. 정말 특이하군요.

L : Chŏriro kŏrŏgapshida.
저리로 걸어갑시다.

W : Chŏ kŏnmurŭn muŏshimnikka?
저 건물은 무엇입니까?

L : Chŏgŏsŭn Kyŏnghoeruimnida. Imgŭmnimi chŏgieső yŏrŏ chungyohan ch'uk'ayŏnŭl pep'ulgŏna, ttonŭn oeguk sonnimŭl majihaessŭmnida.
저것은 경회루입니다. 임금님이 저기에서 여러 중요한 축하연을 베풀거나, 또는 외국 손님을 맞이했습니다.

W : Kŭgŏsŭn chŏngmal ungjanghago arŭmdawa poimnida.
그것은 정말 웅장하고 아름다와 보입니다.

L : Yŏnmotka ŭija-esŏ chom shwiŏ polkkayo?
연못가 의자에서 좀 쉬어 볼까요?

W : Ne, kŭrigo sajindo myŏt chang tchikko shipsŭmnida.
네, 그리고 사진도 몇 장 찍고 싶습니다.

**Mr. Lee :** Yes, let's do that.

**Mr. Williams :** There are so many interesting monuments in this palace.

**Mr. Lee :** There used to be many more.
Let's visit the National Museum next.

**Mr. Williams :** O.K.

(*After the visit*)

**Mr. Williams :** The museum is quite nice.
The collections are impressive.

**Mr. Lee :** I'm glad you liked it.
What did you like most?

**Mr. Williams :** I am fascinated by the Koryo celadons.

**Mr. Lee :** You can buy imitations of most masterpieces if you like.

**Mr. Williams :** That's great. Let's plan a shopping trip one day.

L : Ne, kŭrŏk'e hapshida.
네, 그렇게 합시다.

W : I kung anenŭn aju chaemiinnŭn kinyŏmmuri manssŭmnida.
이 궁 안에는 아주 재미있는 기념물이 많습니다.

L : Chŏnenŭn tŏ manassŭmnida. Taŭmŭn kungnip pangmulgwanŭl ka popshida.
전에는 더 많았읍니다. 다음은 국립 박물관을 가 봅시다.

W : Kŭrŏk'e hapshida. 그렇게 합시다.

(방문 후)

W : Pangmulgwanŭn p'ŏk chossŭmnida.
Sojangp'umdŭri insangjŏgimnida.
박물관은 퍽 좋습니다.
소장품들이 인상적입니다.

L : Maŭme tŭshini kippŭmnida.
Muŏshi kajang choŭsyo ssŭmnikka?
마음에 드시니 기쁩니다.
무엇이 가장 좋으셨습니까?

W : Chŏn Koryŏ chagie maehoktoeŏssumnida.
전 고려 자기에 매혹되었습니다.

L : Manil choahashindamyŏn kŏltchakp'um taebubunŭi mojop'umŭl sal su issŭmnida.
만일 좋아하신다면 걸작품 대부분의 모조품을 살 수 있습니다.

W : Kŭgŏt ch'am chaldwaetkunyo. Syop'ing harŏ tanil kyehoegŭl hanbŏn seupshida.
그것 참 잘됐군요.
쇼핑 하러 다닐 계획을 한번 세웁시다.

## 3. Driving around the Seoul City, the Riverside Drive

**Mr. Williams :** This riverside drive is scenic. How many bridges are there across the Han river, Mr. Lee?

**Mr. Lee :** There are more than 14 now, but we always seem to want more.

* * *

**Mr. Lee :** You'll have the feeling of climbing up in the sky.

We call this drive "Sky Way."

**Mr. Williams :** How it winds around!

**Mr. Lee :** There is even a loop ahead.

**Mr. Williams :** How wonderful to have such an exciting drive right in the heart of Seoul!

## 3. 서울 시내와 강변을 두루 운전하면서

W : I kangbyŏn toronŭn kyŏngch'iga chossŭmnida. I sŏnsaengnim, Han-gange noin tariga myŏt kaeimnikka?

이 강변 도로는 경치가 좋습니다. 이 선생님, 한강에 놓인 다리가 몇 개입니까?

L : Chigŭm yŏl nekeaga nŏmsŭmnida. Kŭrŏna hangsang mojaranŭn kŏt kat'ayo.

지금 열 네개가 넘습니다.
그러나 항상 모자라는 것 같아요.

* * *

L : Hanŭre ollaganŭn nŭkkimil kŏshimnida. Igŏsŭl sŭk'aiweirago purŭmnida.

하늘에 올라가는 느낌일 것입니다. 이것을 스카이웨이라고 부릅니다.

W : Aju ppaengppaeng tonŭn-gunyo!

아주 뺑뺑 도는군요!

L : Ije ruup'ŭdo issŭmnida.

이제 루우프도 있습니다.

W : Sŏul hanbokp'anesŏ iwa kach'i shinnanŭn tŭraibŭrŭl handanŭn kŏsŭn ŏlmana mŏdissŏyo!

서울 한복판에서 이와 같이 신나는 드라이브를 한다는 것은 얼마나 멋있어요!

**Mr. Lee :** It's particularly beautiful in the evening like this. Here we are at the Octagonal pavilion.

**Mr. William :** It's a good spot to take a rest.

**Mr. Lee :** Let's have a cold drink upstairs.

* * *

**Mr. Williams :** Hum, now I have a full view of Seoul below me. I never imagined that Seoul would be so big and so beautiful at night.

**Mr. Lee :** Yes, but Seoul is too crowded.

**Mr. Williams :** That's true. Another glass, Mr. Lee?

**Mr. Lee :** With pleasure.

## 4. In Kyongju

**Mr. Song :** Let's take a sightseeing bus to tour the famous places.

L : Onŭl kat'ŭn chŏnyŏgenŭn t'ŭkpyŏrhi tŏ arŭmdawŏyo. P'algakchŏnge ta wassŭmnida.
오늘 같은 저녁에는 특별히 더 아름다워요.
팔각정에 다 왔습니다.

W : Yŏginŭn shwigi choŭn koshimnida.
여기는 쉬기 좋은 곳입니다.

L : Wich'ŭngesŏ ch'an ŭmnyorŭl mashipshida.
위층에서 찬 음료를 마십시다.

* * *

W : Ŭm, ije Sŏurŭi chŏn-gyŏngi nun arae poinŭn-gunyo. Nanŭn Sŏuri irŏk'e k'ŭgo, tto chŏnyŏge it'orok arŭmdaunji sangsangdo mot'aessŭmnida.
음, 이제 서울의 전경이 눈 아래 보이는군요. 나는 서울이 이렇게 크고, 또 저녁에 이토록 아름다운지 상상도 못했습니다.

L : Ne, kŭrŏna Sŏurŭn nŏmu pumbimnida.
네, 그러나 서울은 너무 붐빕니다.

W : Sashirimnida. Cha, han chan tŏ hashilkkayo, I sŏnsaengnim?
사실입니다. 자, 한 잔 더 하실까요, 이 선생님?

L : Kamsahamnida. 감사합니다.

## 4. 경주에서

S : Kwan-gwang pŏsŭro yumyŏnghan kosŭl kugyŏnghapshida. 관광 버스로 유명한 곳을 구경합시다.

**Mr. Goldsmith :** That'll be fine. What time does the bus start?

**Mr. Song :** The city sightseeing bus leaves at 9 in the morning, and will return by noon for lunch.

**Mr. Goldsmith :** That sounds fine. Then, will we be visiting Pulguksa and Sokkuram in the afternoon?

**Mr. Song :** Yes, the bus leaves at 2 and will return at 6 in the evening.

**Mr. Goldsmith :** I am looking forward to it.

* * *

**Mr. Goldsmith :** When will we have time to visit the new Museum?

**Mr. Song :** We will visit it tomorrow morning.

I am sure two hours is not enough to see everything.

G : Kŭgŏt chok'essŭmnida. Myŏt shie pŏsŭga ch'ulbarhamnikka?
그것 좋겠습니다.
몇 시에 버스가 출발합니까?

S : Shinae kwan-gwang pŏsŭnŭn ach'im ahopshie ch'ulbarhamnida. Kŭrigo chŏmshim mŏgŭrŏ chŏngo kkaji toraomnida.
시내 관광 버스는 아침 아홉시에 출발합니다. 그리고 점심 먹으러 정오까지 돌아옵니다.

G : Kwaench'ank'unyo. Kŭrŏm ohue Pulguksawa Sŏkkuramŭl kugyŏnghage toemnikka?
괜찮군요. 그럼 오후에 불국사와 석굴암을 구경하게 됩니까?

S : Ne, pŏsŭga tushie ttŏna chŏnyŏk yŏsŏssie toraomnida.
네, 버스가 두시에 떠나 저녁 여섯시에 돌아옵니다.

G : Kidaryŏjinŭn-gunyo.
기다려지는군요.

* * *

G : Ŏnje sae pangmulgwanŭl kugyŏnghage toemnikka?
언제 새 박물관을 구경하게 됩니까?

S : Naeil ach'ime poge toemnida. Tu shigan tongane ta pol sunŭn ŏpsŭmnida.
내일 아침에 보게 됩니다. 두 시간 동안에 다 볼 수는 없습니다.

**Mr. Goldsmith :** I'll be willing to devote more time there.

Then, that will conclude our visit of Kyongju, won't it?

**Mr. Song :** That's right. We'll take an express for Pusan tomorrow afternoon at 4. It takes only one hour to get to Pusan.

**Mr. Goldsmith :** Good. Now, let's go down to get on the bus. It's nearly 9 now.

**Mr. Song :** Right.

### 5. At the Restaurant in Pusan

**Mr. Goldsmith :** This shrimp is excellent!

**Mr. Lee :** I'm glad you liked it. I come to this place every time I come to Pusan.

G : Chŏn kŏgiesŏ shiganŭl tŏ ponaedo chossŭmnida. Kŭrŏm Kyŏngju kwan-gwangi kkŭnnage toel kŏshimnida. Kŭrŏch'i anayo?
전 거기에서 시간을 더 보내도 좋습니다. 그럼 경주 관광이 끝나게 될 것입니다.
그렇지 않아요?

S : Kŭraeyo. Naeil ohu neshie Pusan kanŭn kŭp'aengŭl t'amnida. Pusane toch'ak'anŭn te han shiganimyŏn toemnida.
그래요. 내일 오후 네시에 부산 가는 급행을 탑니다. 부산에 도착하는 데 한 시간이면 됩니다.

G : Chossŭmnida.
Cha, pŏsŭ t'arŏ kapshida.
Ahopshiga kŏŭi ta twaessŭmnida.
좋습니다.
자, 버스 타러 갑시다.
아홉시가 거의 다 됐습니다.

S : Kŭrŏk'unyo.
그렇군요.

## 5. 부산 식당에서

G : I saeu aju madissŭmnida.
이 새우 아주 맛있습니다.

L : Choahashini kippŭmnida.
Chŏnŭn Pusan ol ttaemada ikose omnida.
좋아하시니 기쁩니다.
저는 부산 올 때마다 이 곳에 옵니다.

**Mr. Goldsmith :** And their service is quite satisfactory, too. Now, Mr. Lee, wasn't our plane reservation for Cheju-do for 11 tomorrow morning?

**Mr. Lee :** That's right. You can have plenty of sleep tomorrow morning.

**Mr. Goldsmith :** That's a relief. How many days will we be on the Island?

**Mr. Lee :** Three or four days, depending on the weather.
There are so many things to see.

**Mr. Goldsmith :** Let's hope the weather will be fine.

G : Kŭrigo sŏbisŭdo p'ŏk manjoksŭrŏpsŭmnida. Chŏ, I sŏnsaengnim, naeil ach'im Cheju kanŭn pihaenggi yeyagi yŏrhanshijiyo?
그리고 서비스도 퍽 만족스럽습니다. 저, 이 선생님, 내일 아침 제주 가는 비행기 예약이 열한시지요?

L : Kŭrŏssŭmnida. Naeil ach'imkkaji chamŭl ch'ungbunhi chal su issŭmnida.
그렇습니다. 내일 아침까지 잠을 충분히 잘 수 있습니다.

G : Chal shwigessŭmnida. Chejudo-esŏ myŏch'irina itke toelkkayo?
잘 쉬겠읍니다. 제주도에서 며칠이나 있게 될까요?

L : Samirina sairiyo, kihue tallyŏssŭmnida. Pol kŏshi hado manasŏyo.
삼일이나 사일이요, 기후에 달렸습니다. 볼 것이 하도 많아서요.

G : Nalssiga chok'irŭl paramnida.
날씨가 좋기를 바랍니다.

# XIII. HOTEL

## ☐ Useful Expressions

1. I want a single room for tonight, please.
2. We have only twin bed rooms left, sir.
3. I would like a room with bath.
4. I made a reservation.
5. How many days are you going to stay?
6. What is the price of this room?
7. I'll take this room.
8. Is there anything I can do for you?
9. Could you clean my room a little later?
10. Do you accept travellers check?
11. Please have these clothes laundered.
12. How soon will they be ready?

# XIII. 호 텔

## □ 많이 쓰는 표현

1. Onŭl pam ch'imdae hana innŭn pangŭl wŏnhamnida. 오늘 밤 침대 하나 있는 방을 원합니다.
2. Ch'imdae tul innŭn pangman nama issŭmnida. 침대 둘 있는 방만 남아 있습니다.
3. Yokshil innŭn pangŭl wŏnhamnida. 욕실 있는 방을 원합니다.
4. Yeyagŭl haessŭmnida. 예약을 했습니다.
5. Myŏch'ilganina yuhashigessŭmnikka? 며칠간이나 유하시겠습니까?
6. I pangŭi kapsŭn ŏlmaimnikka? 이 방의 값은 얼마입니까?
7. I pangŭl ssŭgessŭmnida. 이 방을 쓰겠습니다.
8. Chega towa tŭril iri issŭmnikka? 제가 도와 드릴 일이 있습니까?
9. Chamshi hue nae pangŭl ch'ŏngsohae chushigessŭmnikka? 잠시 후에 내 방을 청소해 주시겠습니까?
10. Yŏhaengja sup'yorŭl padŭshimnikka? 여행자 수표를 받으십니까?
11. I osŭl set'ak'ae chuseyo. 이 옷을 세탁해 주세요.
12. Ŏlmana ppalli toemnikka? 얼마나 빨리 됩니까?

13. Is there any place where I can get a haircut?

14. When do you begin to serve dinner?

15. At what time will breakfast be ready?

16. Please call a taxi for me.

17. I'll check out now.

18. (Please bring me) My bill, please.

19. Please come again.

20. Thank you. I enjoyed my stay here.

## 1. Hotel(1)

**Mr. Slow :** Excuse me. Where is a good hotel in this town?

**A Passer-by :** Well, I am sure the Susong hotel is the best.

**Mr. Slow :** How can I get there?

13. Mŏri kkakkŭl koshi issŭmnikka?
머리 깎을 곳이 있습니까?
14. Chŏnyŏk shiksanŭn myŏt shie shijak'amnikka?
저녁 식사는 몇 시에 시작합니까?
15. Myŏt shie ach'im shiksaga toemnikka?
몇 시에 아침 식사가 됩니까?
16. T'aekshi chom pullŏ chuseyo.
택시 좀 불러 주세요.
17. Chigŭm nagagessŭmnida.
지금 나가겠습니다.
18. Kyesansŏ kajyŏoseyo.
계산서 가져오세요.
19. Tto oshipshio.
또 오십시오.
20. Kamsahamnida.
Chal mugŏssŭmnida.
감사합니다.
잘 묵었습니다.

## 1. 호 텔 (1)

S : Mianhamnida. Yŏgie choŭn hot'eri ŏdi issŭmnikka?
미안합니다. 여기에 좋은 호텔이 어디 있습니까?

P : Kŭlsseyo, Susong hot'eri cheil chossŭmnida.
글쎄요, 수송 호텔이 제일 좋습니다.

S : Ŏttŏk'e kŏgie kal su issŭmnikka?
어떻게 거기에 갈 수 있습니까?

**A Passer-by :** Go straight ahead and turn right at the first intersection.
Walk down about 100 meters and you will find a five store building on your left, sii. That's the hotel. (*yeogwan*).

**Mr. Slow :** Thank you.

*　　*　　*

**Clerk :** Good evening, sir.

**Mr. Slow :** I want a room for tonight. Do you have one with a good view of the sea?

**Clerk :** Yes, sir. A special room on the fifth floor is vacant now. It is the best one in our hotel.

**Mr. Slow :** How does the special room differ from other rooms?

**Clerk :** Well, a special room is actually a two room suite with private bath.
The first class room is a single room with private bath, and the economy class

P : Ap'ŭro kotchang kasyŏsŏ ch'ŏt kyoch'aro-esŏ orŭntchogŭro toshipshio. Paek mit'ŏtchŭm kŏrŏ naeryŏgamyŏn oentchoge och'ŭng kŏnmuri poimnida. Kŭgŏshi hot'erimnida.
앞으로 곧장 가셔서 첫 교차로에서 오른쪽으로 도십시오. 백 미터쯤 걸어 내려가면 왼쪽에 오층 건물이 보입니다. 그것이 그 호텔입니다.

S : Kamsahamnida.
감사합니다.

* * *

C : Ŏsŏ oshipshio.
어서 오십시오.

S : Onŭl pam chal pangŭl wŏnhamnida. Pada kyŏngch'iga choŭn pang issŭmnikka?
오늘 밤 잘 방을 원합니다. 바다 경치가 좋은 방 있습니까?

C : Ne, och'ŭnge t'ukshiri chigŭm piŏ issŭmnida. Kŭgŏshi uri yŏgwanesŏ cheil choŭn pangimnida.
네, 오층에 특실이 지금 비어 있습니다. 그것이 우리 여관에서 제일 좋은 방입니다.

S : T'ŭkshiri tarŭn panggwa ŏttŏk'e tarŭmnikka?
특실이 다른 방과 어떻게 다릅니까?

C : Ne, t'ŭkshirŭn shilchero yokshirŭl katch'un tu pangtchariimnida. Iltŭngshirŭn pang hana-e yokshiri itko, pot'ongbangŭn kongdong yokshiri issŭmnida. T'ukshirina iltŭngshire ondolgwa yang-

has a common floor bath. We have both *ondol* and western style rooms in the special and the first class rooms.

**Mr. Slow :** I would like a special room, *ondol*.

How much is it a day?

**Clerk :** It's 70,000 won, sir.

**Mr. Slow :** That's fine. Can I see the room?

**Clerk :** Yes, sir. This way, please.

## 2. Hotel (2)

**Clerk :** Good afternoon, sir.

**Mr. Song :** Good afternoon. I made a reservation for two rooms. My name is Song In Ho.

**Clerk :** Yes, sir. They are room 306 and 309 on the third floor.

**Mr. Williams :** Are the rooms quiet?

shiri ta issŭmnida.
네, 특실은 실제로 욕실을 갖춘 두 방짜리입니다. 일등실은 방 하나에 욕실이 있고, 보통방은 공동 욕실이 있읍니다. 특실이나 일등실에 온돌과 양실이 다 있습니다.

S : T'ŭkshil ondorŭl ssŭgessŭmnida. Harue ŏlmaimnikka?
특실 온돌을 쓰겠습니다. 하루에 얼마입니까?

C : Ch'ilmanwŏnimnida.
칠만원입니다.

S : Chossŭmnida. Pangŭl pol su issŭlkkayo?
좋습니다. 방을 볼 수 있을까요?

C : Ne, iriro oshipshio.
네, 이리로 오십시오.

## 2. 호 텔(2)

C : Ŏsŏ oshipshio.
어서 오십시오.

S : Annyŏnghashimnikka. Pang turŭl yeyak'aessŭmnida. Che irŭmŭn Song In-hoimnida.
안녕하십니까. 방 둘을 예약했습니다. 제 이름은 송인호입니다.

C : Ne, samch'unge sambaengyuk'owa sambaekkuhoshirimnida.
네, 삼층에 삼백육호와 삼백구호실입니다.

W : Pangi choyonghamnikka?
방이 조용합니까?

**Clerk :** Yes, sir. They face the back street, so they are very quite and cozy.

**Mr. Williams :** I would like to see the rooms.

**Clerk :** Yes, sir. This way, please.

* * *

**Mr. Williams :** I think the rooms are all right. What do you think, Mr. Song?

**Mr. Song :** They're nice. Will you take this room?

**Mr. Williams :** Yes, I like it.

**Clerk :** I will have your baggage sent up right away.

**Mr. Song :** By the way, how much is the room a day?

**Clerk :** It's 11,000 won. The price is posted on the door here.

C : Ne, pangi kŏri twitchogŭro na issŏ aju choyŏng-hago anŭk'amnida.
네, 방이 거리 뒤쪽으로 나 있어 아주 조용하고 아늑합니다.

W : Pangŭl pogo shipsŭmnida.
방을 보고 싶습니다.

C : Ne, iriro oshipshio.
네, 이리로 오십시오.

*　　*　　*

W : Pangi maŭme tŭmnida.
Song sŏnsaengnimŭn ŏttŏseyo?
방이 마음에 듭니다.
송 선생님은 어떠세요?

S : Chossŭmnida. I pang ssŭshigessŭmnikka?
좋습니다. 이 방 쓰시겠습니까?

W : Ne, i pangi maŭme tŭmnida.
네, 이 방이 마음에 듭니다.

C : Chimŭl kot ollyŏ ponae tŭrigessŭmnida.
짐을 곧 올려 보내 드리겠습니다.

S : Kŭrŏnde, i pang harue ŏlmaimnikka?
그런데 이 방 하루에 얼마입니까?

C : Manch'ŏnwŏnimnida. Pangkapsŭn mune puch'yŏ issŭmnida. Yŏlsoe padŭseyo. I yongjie kirok'ashi-go naeryŏoshil ttae p'ŭrŏnt'ŭ tesŭk'ŭe katta chu-shipshio.
만천원입니다. 방값은 문에 붙여 있습니다. 열쇠 받으

Here're your keys. Please fill in these forms and leave them at the front desk when you come down.

**Mr. Song :** All right.

### 3. At the Front Desk

**Mr. Williams :** Here's the forms filled out.

**Clerk :** Thank you, sir.

**Mr. Williams :** By the way, where is the dining room?

**Clerk :** It's over there, on your right, sir. There's another one on the 15th floor. It's a sky lounge with a good view.

**Mr. Williams :** Good. I may try there in the evening. Is there a barber shop in this hotel?

**Clerk :** Yes, it's in the basement. It's open until 8 in the evening.

**Mr. Williams :** That's very convenient.

세요. 이 용지에 기록하시고 내려오실 때 프런트 데스크에 갖다 주십시오.

S : Arassŭmnida.
알았읍니다.

## 3. 프런트 데스크에서

W : Ta kiip'aessŭmnida.
다 기입했읍니다.

C : Kamsahamnida.
감사합니다.

W : Kŭrŏnde shiktangi ŏdi issŭmnikka?
그런데, 식당이 어디 있습니까?

C : Chŏgi orŭnp'yŏne issŭmnida. Shiboch'ŭnge tto hana issŭmnida. Sŭk'ai raunjiigi ttaemune kyŏngch'iga chossŭmnida.
저기 오른편에 있습니다. 십오층에 또 하나 있습니다. 스카이 라운지이기 때문에 경치가 좋습니다.

W : Chossŭmnida. Chŏnyŏge kŏgirŭl ka pogessŭmnida. I hot'ere ibalgwani issŭmnikka?
좋습니다. 저녁에 거기를 가 보겠습니다. 이 호텔에 이발관이 있습니까?

C : Ne, chihashire issŭmnida.
Chŏnyŏk yŏdŏlshikkajiimnida.
네, 지하실에 있습니다.
저녁 여덟시까지입니다.

W : Aju p'yŏllihagunyo.
아주 편리하군요.

**Clerk** : We have also several souvenir shops in the basement.

There are quite a variety, and you may want to take a look at them.

**Mr. Williams** : Thank you.

## 4. In the Hotel Room

**Bellboy** : Yes, sir. What can I do for you?

**Mr. Williams** : I would like to have these shirts and socks washed.

**Bellboy** : Yes, sir.

**Mr. Williams** : And have this pair of pants pressed, please.

How soon will they be ready?

**Bellboy** : The pants can be pressed right away, but the shirts will be ready tomorrow morning.

**Mr. Williams** : That's fine.

C : Ttohan chihashirenŭn kinyŏmp'um sangjŏmdo myŏt issŭmnida.
Yŏrŏ kajiga issŏsŏ, hanbŏn ka poshil manhamnida.
또한 지하실에는 기념품 상점도 몇 있습니다.
여러 가지가 있어서, 한번 가 보실 만합니다.

W : Kamsahamnida.
감사합니다.

## 4. 호텔 방에서

B : Ne. Muŏsŭl towa tŭrilkkayo?
네.
무엇을 도와 드릴까요?

W : I syassŭwa yangmarŭl ppalgo ship'ŭndeyo.
이 샤쓰와 양말을 빨고 싶은데요.

B : Ne.
네.

W : Kŭrigo i pajirŭl taryŏ chushipshio.
Ŏlmana ppalli toelkkayo?
그리고 이 바지를 다려 주십시오.
얼마나 빨리 될까요?

B : Pajinŭn kot taril su issŭmnidaman syassŭnŭn naeil ach'ime toegessŭmnida.
바지는 곧 다릴 수 있습니다만 샤쓰는 내일 아침에 되겠습니다.

W : Choayo.
좋아요.

**Bellboy** : Anything else, sir?

**Mr. Williams** : Is there a quick dry cleaning service?

I want these suits dry cleaned.

**Bellboy** : Yes, sir. We have a 3 hour dry cleaning service.

**Mr. Williams** : Then take these suits to be cleaned, too.

**Bellboy** : Yes, sir.

Seoul Plaza Hotel

B : Tto tarŭn kŏsŭn ŏpsŭmnikka?
또 다른 것은 없습니까?

W : Ppalli toenŭn tŭrai k'ŭlliningi issŏyo?
I yangbogŭl tŭraihago ship'ŭndeyo.
빨리 되는 드라이 클리닝이 있어요? 이 양복을 드라이 하고 싶은데요.

B : Ne, issŭmnida. Se shigane toenŭn dŭrai k'ŭlliningi issŭmnida.
네 있습니다. 세 시간에 되는 드라이 클리닝이 있습니다.

W : Kŭrŏm i yangbokto tŭraihae chuseyo.
그럼 이 양복도 드라이해 주세요.

B : Ne, arassŭmnida.
네, 알았습니다.

Chosun Hotel

# XIV. WEATHER AND SEASONS

## ☐ Useful Expressions

1. It is fine today.
2. It was cloudy and very windy yesterday.
3. It's a typical warm spring day today. It gets sometimes foggy, too.
4. Does it rain a lot in spring?
5. When is the hottest month in Korea?
6. I like best the dry cool weather in the fall.
7. How cold does it get in winter?
8. Does it snow in Korea, too?
9. There are four definite seasons in Korea.
10. Summer is hot and it rains often.

# XIV. 기후와 계절

## □ 많이 쓰는 표현

1. Onŭrŭn nalssiga chossŭmnida.
   오늘은 날씨가 좋습니다.
2. Ŏjenŭn hŭrigo parami mani purŏssŭmnida.
   어제는 흐리고 바람이 많이 불었습니다.
3. Onŭrŭn chŏnhyŏngjŏgin ttattŭt'an pomnarimnida. Kakkŭm an-gaedo kkimnida.
   오늘은 전형적인 따뜻한 봄날입니다. 가끔 안개도 낍니다.
4. Pome piga mani omnikka?
   봄에 비가 많이 옵니까?
5. Han-gugesŏ kajang tŏun tari ŏnjeimnikka?
   한국에서 가장 더운 달이 언제입니까?
6. Nanŭn kaŭrŭi kŏnjohago shiwŏnhan kyejŏrŭl cheil choahamnida.
   나는 가을의 건조하고 시원한 계절을 제일 좋아합니다.
7. Kyŏurenŭn ŏlmana ch'uwŏjimnikka?
   겨울에는 얼마나 추워집니까?
8. Han-gugedo nuni omnikka?
   한국에도 눈이 옵니까?
9. Han-gugenŭn sagyejŏri tturyŏt'amnida.
   한국에는 사계절이 뚜렷합니다.
10. Yŏrŭmŭn tŏpko chaju piga omnida.
    여름은 덥고 자주 비가 옵니다.

* * *

A : What a beautiful day!

B : Yes, you can't hope for any better.

A : There is not even a breeze.

B : Yes, and the sunshine is comfortable.

A : But, aren't you expecting the rainy season soon?

B : Yes. Then, it will rain for a fairly long time.

A : How long does it usually rain?

B : Oh, about a month or so. Still, we'll have very hot weather for sometime.

A : Then I had better go to the sea.

* * *

A : It is damp and cloudy. We may have rain

* * *

A : Nalssiga ch'am chok'unyo! 날씨가 참 좋군요!
B : Ne, tŏ paral kŏshi ŏpsŭmnida.
네, 더 바랄 것이 없습니다.
A : Parami chogŭmdo ŏpsŏyo.
바람이 조금도 없어요.
B : Ne, kŭrigo haetpyŏch'i p'ogŭnhamnida.
네, 그리고 햇볕이 포근합니다.
A : Hajiman kot changmaga onŭn kŏt animnikka?
하지만 곧 장마가 오는 것 아닙니까?
B : Ne, kŭrŏmyŏn kkwae oraettongan piga omnida.
네, 그러면 꽤 오랫동안 비가 옵니다.
A : Pot'ong ŏlma tongan piga omnikka?
보통 얼마 동안 비가 옵니까?
B : Ah, yak han taltchŭm omnida. Kŭrigodo nalssiga ŏlma tongan maeu tŏpsŭmnida.
아, 약 한 달쯤 옵니다. 그리고도 날씨가 얼마 동안 매우 덥습니다.
A : Kŭrŏm pada-ena kanŭn kŏshi chok'etkunyo.
그럼 바다에나 가는 것이 좋겠군요.

* * *

A : Nalssiga mudŏpko hŭryŏssŭmnida. Kot piga ogessŭmnida. Ilgi yebonŭn muŏrago haessŏyo?
날씨가 무덥고 흐렸습니다. 곧 비가 오겠습니다. 일기 예보는 무어라고 했어요?

soon. What did the weather forecast say?

**B** : It said it will rain in the afternoon, but will clear up by tomorrow morning.

**A** : Oh, I am saved. We are planning to go on a picnic tomorrow and I was worried.

**B** : The bad weather doesn't last long in this season. We have a lot of sunny days.

**A** : Good, I want to enjoy the outdoors as much as I can.

**B** : I am sure you won't be disappointed.

* * *

**A** : It is a pleasant cool day, isn't it? The sky is so blue.
Not even a patch of cloud in the sky, and the air is so dry.

**B** : Yes, I like the fall best and it is a typical fall day in Korea.

**B** : Ohuenŭn piga ona naeil ach'imkkajinŭn kael kŏshira hayŏssŭmnida.
오후에는 비가 오나 내일 아침까지는 갤 것이라 하였습니다.

**A** : Ah, chal twaessŭmnida. Urinŭn naeil sop'ung kal kyehoegira kŭnshimhaessŭmnida.
아, 잘 됐습니다. 우리는 내일 소풍 갈 계획이라 근심했습니다.

**B** : I kyejŏrenŭn nappŭn nalssiga orae kaji anssŭmnida. Hae nanŭn nari manssŭmnida.
이 계절에는 나쁜 날씨가 오래 가지 않습니다. 해 나는 날이 많습니다.

**A** : Chossŭmnida. Chŏnŭn toedorok ya-oeesŏ chŭlgigo shipsŭmnida.
좋습니다. 저는 되도록 야외에서 즐기고 싶습니다.

**B** : Ama shilmanghaji anŭl kŏmnida.
아마 실망하지 않을 겁니다.

* * *

**A** : Kibunjok'e shiwŏnhan narimnida. Kŭrŏch'iyo? Hanŭri ŏtchina p'urŭnjiyo. Hanŭre kurŭm han chŏm ŏpko konggiga aju kŏnjohamnida.
기분좋게 시원한 날입니다. 그렇지요? 하늘이 어찌나 푸른지요. 하늘에 구름 한 점 없고 공기가 아주 건조합니다.

**B** : Ne, chŏnŭn kaŭrŭl cheil choahaeyo.
Kŭrigo igŏshi Han-gugŭi chŏnhyŏngjŏgin kaŭl-

A : How long does the fall last in Korea?

B : About three months.

But sometimes the winter comes earlier than usual.

Then, it gets quite cold even in the beginning of December.

* * *

A : How cold does it get in winter?

B : The average is about 6 degrees below zero centigrade, but the coldest day in Seoul may be drop as low as 17 degrees or 18 degrees below zero.

A : That's quite cold. Does it snow here, too?

B : Yes, but not very much recently.

A : Well, I like snow. I'll be looking forward to it.

larimnida. 네, 저는 가을을 제일 좋아해요. 그리고 이것이 한국의 전형적인 가을날입니다.

A : Han-gugesŏnŭn kaŭri ŏlma tongan kyesoktoemnikka?
한국에서는 가을이 얼마 동안 계속됩니까?

B : Yak sŏk tal kamnida. Kŭrŏna ttaeronŭn kyŏuri pot'ongttaeboda iltchik omnida. Kŭrŏmyŏn shibiwŏlch'o-edo chebŏp ch'upsŭmnida.
약 석 달 갑니다. 그러나 때로는 겨울이 보통때보다 일찍 옵니다. 그러면 십이월초에도 제법 춥습니다.

* * *

A : Kyŏurenŭn ŏlmana ch'uwŏjimnikka?
겨울에는 얼마나 추워집니까?

B : P'yŏnggyun yak sŏpssi yŏngha yuktoimnidaman, Sŏuresŏ kajang ch'uun narŭn yŏngha shipch'iltona shipp'altokkajido naeryŏgamnida.
평균 약 섭씨 영하 육도입니다만, 서울에서 가장 추운 날은 영하 십칠도나 십팔도까지도 내려갑니다.

A : Sangdanghi ch'upkunyo. Nundo omnikka?
상당히 춥군요. 눈도 옵니까?

B : Ne, kŭrŏnde kŭllaeenŭn pyŏllo mani oji anssŭmnida.
네, 그런데 근래에는 별로 많이 오지 않습니다.

A : Kŭraeyo, chŏnŭn nunŭl ch'am choahamnida. Kidaryŏjimnida.
그래요, 저는 눈을 참 좋아합니다. 기다려집니다.

# PART III

# VOCABULARIES

## TIME

### 때 (Ttae)

| | | |
|---|---|---|
| second | ch'o | 초 |
| minute | pun | 분 |
| o'clock | shi | 시 |
| hour | shigan | 시간 |
| day | nal | 날 |
| morning | ach'im | 아침 |
| noon | chŏngo | 정오 |
| evening | chŏnyŏk | 저녁 |
| forenoon | ojŏn | 오전 |
| afternoon | ohu | 오후 |
| night | pam | 밤 |
| midnight | chajŏng | 자정 |
| today | onŭl | 오늘 |
| tomorrow | naeil | 내일 |
| yesterday | ŏje | 어제 |
| the other day | yojŏnnal | 요전날 |
| some day | ŏttŏn nal | 어떤 날 |
| week | chu | 주 |
| month | tal | 달 |
| birthday | saengil | 생일 |
| year | hae | 해 |
| this morning | onŭl ach'im | 오늘 아침 |
| tonight | onŭl pam | 오늘 밤 |
| this week | ibŏn chuil | 이번 주일 |
| next week | taŭm chuil | 다음 주일 |
| last week | chinan chuil | 지난 주일 |

| | | |
|---|---|---|
| this month | idal | 이달 |
| next month | taŭmtal | 다음달 |
| last month | chinandal | 지난달 |
| this year | orhae(ihae) | 올해(이해) |
| last year | chinanhae | 지난해 |
| next year | taŭmhae | 다음해 |
| present time | hyŏnjae | 현재 |
| future time | mirae | 미래 |
| weekend | chumal | 주말 |
| early | iltchigi | 일찌기 |
| soon | kot | 곧 |
| late | nŭtke | 늦게 |
| just | kkok | 꼭 |

## WEATHER AND SEASON
## 기후와 계절(Kihuwa Kyejŏl)

| | | |
|---|---|---|
| Central Meteorological Observatory | chungang kisangdae | 중앙 기상대 |
| weather forecast | ilgi yebo | 일기 예보 |
| average temperature | p'yŏnggyun ondo | 평균 온도 |
| four definite seasons | sagyejŏl | 사계절 |
| fine (nice) day | kaen nal | 갠 날 |
| raining day | pionŭn nal | 비오는 날 |
| bad (cloudy, nasty) day | hŭrin nal | 흐린 날 |
| warm (hot) day | tŏun nal | 더운 날 |
| cool | sŏnŭrhan | 서늘한 |
| comfortable | p'ogŭnhan | 포근한 |
| dry | kŏnjohan | 건조한 |
| windy | param punŭn | 바람 부는 |

| | | |
|---|---|---|
| drizzle | isŭlbi | 이슬비 |
| downpour | p'ogu | 폭우 |
| favorable wind | sunp'ung | 순풍 |
| gale | chilp'ung | 질풍 |
| drought | kamum | 가뭄 |
| freeze | ŏlda | 얼다 |
| dew | isŭl | 이슬 |
| rainbow | mujigae | 무지개 |
| fog | an-gae | 안개 |
| snow | nun | 눈 |
| ice | ŏrŭm | 얼음 |
| frost | sŏri | 서리 |
| lightning | pŏn-gae | 번개 |
| thunder | ch'ŏndung | 천둥 |
| haze | ajiraengi | 아지랭이 |
| early spring | irŭnbom | 이른봄 |
| last spring | nŭjŭnbom | 늦은봄 |
| midsummer | hanyŏrŭm | 한여름 |
| the rainy season | changmach'ŏl | 장마철 |
| glaring sun | p'ogyŏm | 폭염 |
| spring | pom | 봄 |
| summer | yŏrŭm | 여름 |
| autumn, fall | kaŭl | 가을 |
| winter | kyŏul | 겨울 |
| vernal equinox | ch'unbun | 춘분 |
| summer solstice | haji | 하지 |
| dog days | sambok | 삼복 |
| sweltering heat | taesŏ | 대서 |
| the first day of fall | ipch'u | 입추 |
| autumnal equinox | ch'ubun | 추분 |

| | | |
|---|---|---|
| winter solstice | tongji | 동지 |
| the solar calendar | yangnyŏk | 양력 |
| the lunar calendar | ŭmnyŏk | 음력 |

## MEALS
식사 (Shiksa)

| | | |
|---|---|---|
| rice | pap | 밥 |
| soup | kuk | 국 |
| drink | ŭmnyo | 음료 |
| small sidedishes | panch'an | 반찬 |
| breakfast | choban | 조반 |
| lunch | chŏmshim | 점심 |
| supper | chŏnyŏk | 저녁 |
| Korean dinner | hanjŏngshik | 한정식 |
| Korean dishes | Han-guk yori | 한국 요리 |
| Western dishes | sŏyang yori | 서양 요리 |
| Chinese dishes | Chungguk yori | 중국 요리 |
| Japanese dishes | Ilbon yori | 일본 요리 |
| meat | kogi | 고기 |
| beef | soegogi | 쇠고기 |
| pork | twaejigogi | 돼지고기 |
| chicken | takkogi | 닭고기 |
| roast meat | pulgogi | 불고기 |
| fish | saengsŏn | 생선 |
| fried shrimp | saeu t'wigim | 새우 튀김 |
| egg | talgyal | 달걀 |
| vegetable soup | yach'aekuk | 야채국 |
| fish soup | saengsŏnkuk | 생선국 |
| pickle | kimch'i | 김치 |

| | | |
|---|---|---|
| bread | ppang | 빵 |
| milk | uyu | 우유 |
| coffee | K'ŏp'i | 커피 |
| black tea | hongch'a | 홍차 |
| ginger tea | saenggangch'a | 생강차 |
| ginseng tea | insamch'a | 인삼차 |
| beer | maekchu | 맥주 |
| (grape) wine | p'odoju | 포도주 |
| fruits | kwail | 과일 |
| apple | sagwa | 사과 |
| pear | pae | 배 |
| strawberry | ttalgi | 딸기 |
| watermelon | subak | 수박 |
| peach | poksunga | 복숭아 |
| grape | p'odo | 포도 |
| orange | kyul | 귤 |
| melon | ch'amoe | 참외 |
| condiments | yangnyŏm | 양념 |
| sugar | sŏlt'ang | 설탕 |
| salt | sogŭm | 소금 |
| soy sauce | kanjang | 간장 |
| pepper | huch'u | 후추 |
| red pepper | koch'u | 고추 |
| mustard | kyŏja | 겨자 |
| vinegar | ch'o | 초 |
| menu | menyu | 메뉴 |
| cook | yorisa | 요리사 |
| waiter | kŭpsa | 급사 |
| waitress | yŏgŭp | 여급 |
| appetite | shigyok | 식욕 |

| | | |
|---|---|---|
| meal ticket | shikkwŏn | 식권 |

## HOUSE
집(Chip)

| | | |
|---|---|---|
| residence | chut'aek | 주택 |
| mansion | chŏt'aek | 저택 |
| European house | yangok | 양옥 |
| Korean-style house | hanok | 한옥 |
| apartment complex | ap'at'ŭ | 아파트 |
| rented house | setchip | 셋집 |
| boardinghouse | hasukchip | 하숙집 |
| villa | pyŏlchang | 별장 |
| address | chuso | 주소 |
| house number | pŏnji | 번지 |
| gate | taemun | 대문 |
| entrance | ipku | 입구 |
| fence | tam | 담 |
| roof | chibung | 지붕 |
| first floor(ground floor) | ilch'ŭng | 일층 |
| second floor | ich'ŭng | 이층 |
| step | ch'ŭngch'ŭngdae | 층층대 |
| stairway | kyedan | 계단 |
| window | ch'angmun | 창문 |
| door | mun | 문 |
| kitchen | puŏk | 부엌 |
| kitchenette | chubang | 주방 |
| study | sŏjae | 서재 |
| toilet | pyŏnso | 변소 |
| bathroom | yokshil | 욕실 |

| | | |
|---|---|---|
| floor | maru | 마루 |
| ceiling | ch'ŏnjang | 천장 |
| portico | hyŏn-gwan | 현관 |
| western-style room | yangshil | 양실 |
| basement | chihashil | 지하실 |
| balustrade | nan-gan | 난간 |
| chimney | kulttuk | 굴뚝 |
| drawing room | ŭngjŏpshil | 응접실 |
| dining room | shiktang | 식당 |
| sitting room | anpang | 안방 |
| bedroom | ch'imshil | 침실 |
| yard | ttŭl | 뜰 |
| greenhouse | onshil | 온실 |
| flower bed | hwadan | 화단 |
| garden | chŏngwŏn | 정원 |
| lawn | chandi | 잔디 |
| landscape | chŏnmang | 전망 |
| enclosure | kunae | 구내 |
| pond | yŏnmot | 연못 |
| fountain | punsu | 분수 |

## FURNITURE
가구(Kagu)

| | | |
|---|---|---|
| shelf | sŏnban | 선반 |
| lamp | chŏndŭng | 전등 |
| vase | kkotpyŏng | 꽃병 |
| brazier | hwaro | 화로 |
| tray | chaengban | 쟁반 |
| tobacco tray | tambaehap | 담배합 |

| | | |
|---|---|---|
| ash tray | chaettŏri | 재떨이 |
| broom | pi | 비 |
| duster | ch'ongch'ae | 총채 |
| waste basket | hyujit'ong | 휴지통 |
| carpet | yungdan | 융단 |
| mattress | yo | 요 |
| stationary bureau | ch'aekchang | 책장 |
| desk | ch'aeksang | 책상 |
| table | t'eibŭl | 테이블 |
| bench | kin ŭija | 긴 의자 |
| stool | kŏlsang | 걸상 |
| armchair | allak ŭija | 안락 의자 |
| dressing table | hwajangdae | 화장대 |
| mirrorstand | kyŏngdae | 경대 |
| chest | chang | 장 |
| cupboard | ch'anchang | 찬장 |
| blind | ch'ail | 차일 |
| electric fan | sŏnp'unggi | 선풍기 |
| fan | puch'ae | 부채 |
| refrigerator | naengjanggo | 냉장고 |

## SHOPPING
### 쇼 핑(Syop'ing)

| | | |
|---|---|---|
| department store | paek'wajŏm | 백화점 |
| market | shijang | 시장 |
| bookstore | ch'aekpang (sŏjŏm) | 책방(서점) |
| jeweler's store | kwigŭmsoksang | 귀금속상 |
| souvenir shop | kinyŏmp'umsang | 기념품상 |
| curio shop | koltongp'umsang | 골동품상 |

| | | |
|---|---|---|
| fancy goods store | yangp'umjŏm | 양품점 |
| shoemaker's | yanghwajŏm | 양화점 |
| optician's | an-gyŏngjŏm | 안경점 |
| baker's | ppangchip (chegwajŏm) | 빵집 (제과점) |
| drugstore | yakkuk | 약국 |
| gift | sŏnmul | 선물 |
| tax-free goods | myŏnsep'um | 면세품 |
| brassware | yugi chep'um | 유기 제품 |
| art works | misulp'um | 미술품 |
| masterpieces | kŏlchakp'um | 걸작품 |
| imitations | mojop'um | 모조품 |
| salesgirl | yŏjŏmwŏn | 여점원 |
| fixed prices | chŏngch'al kagyŏk | 정찰 가격 |
| price list | chŏngkap'yo | 정가표 |
| receipt | yŏngsujŭng | 영수증 |
| change | kŏsŭrŭmton | 거스름돈 |
| wrapping paper | p'ojangji | 포장지 |
| the year-end bargain sale | yŏnmal taemaech'ul | 연말 대매출 |
| clearance sale | ttŏri p'algi | 떨이 팔기 |

## MAN AND HUMAN BODY

사람과 인체(Saramgwa Inch'e)

| | | |
|---|---|---|
| man | saram(namja) | 사람(남자) |
| woman | yŏja | 여자 |
| baby | agi (yua) | 아기(유아) |
| child, kid | ŏrini | 어린이 |
| boy, lad | sonyŏn | 소년 |
| girl | sonyŏ | 소녀 |

| | | |
|---|---|---|
| lass | chŏlmŭn yŏja | 젊은 여자 |
| youth | ch'ŏngnyŏn (chŏlmŭni) | 청년 (젊은이) |
| maid | ch'ŏnyŏ | 처녀 |
| bachelor | ch'onggak | 총각 |
| gentleman | shinsa | 신사 |
| lady | sungnyŏ | 숙녀 |
| bride | shinbu | 신부 |
| bridegroom | shillang | 신랑 |
| ancestor | chosang | 조상 |
| grandfather | harabŏji | 할아버지 |
| grandmother | halmŏni | 할머니 |
| family | kajok | 가족 |
| parents | pumo | 부모 |
| father | abŏji | 아버지 |
| mother | ŏmŏni | 어머니 |
| elder brother | hyŏng | 형 |
| elder sister | ŏnni(nuna) | 언니(누나) |
| younger brother | tongsaeng(au) | 동생(아우) |
| younger sister | nuidongsaeng | 누이동생 |
| descendant | chason | 자손 |
| son | adŭl | 아들 |
| daughter | ttal | 딸 |
| grandson | sonja | 손자 |
| relative | ch'inch'ŏk | 친척 |
| uncle | ajŏssi | 아저씨 |
| aunt | ajumŏni | 아주머니 |
| nephew | chok'a | 조카 |
| niece | chok'attal | 조카딸 |
| husband | namp'yŏn | 남편 |

| | | |
|---|---|---|
| wife | anae | 아내 |
| daughter-in-law | myŏnŭri | 며느리 |
| son-in-law | sawi | 사위 |
| father-in-law | changin | 장인 |
| mother-in-law | changmo | 장모 |
| friend | ch'in-gu | 친구 |
| master | chuin | 주인 |
| employer | koyongin | 고용인 |
| head | mŏri | 머리 |
| face | ŏlgul | 얼굴 |
| forehead | ima | 이마 |
| eyebrow | nunssŏp | 눈썹 |
| eye | nun | 눈 |
| nose | k'o | 코 |
| mouth | ip | 입 |
| lip | ipsul | 입술 |
| cheek | ppyam | 뺨 |
| ear | kwi | 귀 |
| tongue | hyŏ | 혀 |
| throat | mokkumŏng | 목구멍 |
| moustache | kossuyŏm | 콧수염 |
| sideburns | kurenarut | 구레나룻 |
| neck | mok | 목 |
| shoulder | ŏkkae | 어깨 |
| arm | p'al | 팔 |
| elbow | p'alkkumch'i | 팔꿈치 |
| limbs | sujok | 수족 |
| hand | son | 손 |
| wrist | sonmok | 손목 |
| palm | sonpadak | 손바닥 |

| | | |
|---|---|---|
| finger | sonkarak | 손가락 |
| nail | sont'op | 손톱 |
| chest | kasŭm | 가슴 |
| heart | shimjang | 심장 |
| lungs | p'ye | 폐 |
| breast | yubang | 유방 |
| stomach | wi | 위 |
| intestine | chang | 장 |
| loin | hŏri | 허리 |
| back | tŭng | 등 |
| leg | tari | 다리 |
| toe | palkarak | 발가락 |
| foot | pal | 발 |
| ancle | palmok | 발목 |
| heel | paldwikkumch'i | 발뒤꿈치 |
| muscle | kŭnyuk | 근육 |
| bone | pp'yŏ | 뼈 |
| skin | p'ibu | 피부 |
| breath | hohŭp | 호흡 |
| pulse | maekpak | 맥박 |
| senses | kamgak | 감각 |
| sight | shiryŏk | 시력 |
| hearing | ch'ŏnggak | 청각 |
| smell | hugak | 후각 |
| taste | migak | 미각 |
| touch | ch'okkak | 촉각 |
| health | kŏn-gang | 건강 |

## TRAFFIC
### 교 통(Kyot'ong)

| | | |
|---|---|---|
| country road | shigolkil | 시골길 |
| short cut | chirŭmkil | 지름길 |
| side walk | indo | 인도 |
| road way | ch'ado | 차도 |
| pavement | p'odo | 포도 |
| express way | kosok toro | 고속 도로 |
| crossing | negŏri | 네거리 |
| corner | mot'ungi | 모퉁이 |
| tunnel | chihado(kul) | 지하도(굴) |
| subway | chihach'ŏl | 지하철 |
| ascent | kogae | 고개 |
| bridge | tari | 다리 |
| railroad | ch'ŏlto | 철도 |
| car | chadongch'a | 자동차 |
| taxi | t'aekshi | 택시 |
| train | kich'a | 기차 |
| bus | pŏsŭ | 버스 |
| express bus | kosok pŏsŭ | 고속 버스 |
| bicycle | chajŏn-gŏ | 자전거 |
| airplane | pihaenggi | 비행기 |
| ship | pae | 배 |
| driver | kisa(unjŏnsa) | 기사(운전사) |
| drunk driving | ŭmchu unchŏn | 음주운전 |
| bus stop | pŏsŭ chŏngnyujang | 버스 정류장 |
| parking lot | chuch'ajang | 주차장 |
| no parking | chuch'a kŭmji | 주차 금지 |

| | | |
|---|---|---|
| road under repair | toro surijung | 도로 수리중 |
| traffic light | shinhodŭng | 신호등 |
| landmark | kyŏnggyep'yo | 경계표 |
| limited area | t'onghaeng kŭmji kuyŏk | 통행 금지 구역 |
| slow down | ch'ŏnch'ŏnhi | 천천히 |
| stop sign | chŏngji shinho | 정지 신호 |
| speed limit | sokto chehan | 속도 제한 |
| traffic cop | kyot'ong sun-gyŏng | 교통 순경 |
| service station | chadongch'a chuyuso | 자동차 주유소 |

## SIGHTSEEING
### 관 광(Kwan-gwang)

| | | |
|---|---|---|
| tour | yŏhaeng | 여행 |
| passport | yŏkwŏn | 여권 |
| tourist map | kwan-gwang chido | 관광 지도 |
| traveller's check | yŏhaengja sup'yo | 여행자 수표 |
| permission | hŏga | 허가 |
| night tour | yagan kwan-gwang | 야간 관광 |
| tour guide | yŏhaeng annaesŏ | 여행 안내서 |
| sightseeing bus | kwan-gwang pŏsŭ | 관광 버스 |
| dining car | shiktangch'a | 식당차 |
| leave | ch'ulbarhada | 출발하다 |
| get to | toch'ak'ada | 도착하다 |
| fare | yogŭm | 요금 |
| reservation | yeyak | 예약 |
| bill | kyesansŏ | 계산서 |
| round trip ticket | wangbokp'yo | 왕복표 |

| | | |
|---|---|---|
| first class ticket | iltŭngp'yo | 일등표 |
| second class ticket | idŭngp'yo | 이등표 |
| hotel | yŏgwan | 여관 |
| special room | t'ukshil | 특실 |
| single bed | irinyong ch'imdae | 일인용 침대 |
| double bed | iinyong ch'imdae | 이인용 침대 |
| lavatory | semyŏnso | 세면소 |
| hotel charge | sukpakpi | 숙박비 |
| valuables | kwijungp'um | 귀중품 |

## CLOTHING AND PERSONAL ORNAMENT

옷과 장신구(Otkwa Changshin-gu)

| | | |
|---|---|---|
| tailor shop | yangbokchŏm | 양복점 |
| tailormades | mach'umot | 마춤옷 |
| readymade suit | kisŏngbok | 기성복 |
| sport suit | undongbok | 운동복 |
| riding dress | sŭngmabok | 승마복 |
| dress suit | yahoebok | 야회복 |
| wedding gown | hollyebok | 혼례복 |
| uniform | chebok | 제복 |
| military uniform | kunbok | 군복 |
| slacks | chagŏppok | 작업복 |
| party dress | p'at'i tŭresŭ | 파티 드레스 |
| suit | yangbok | 양복 |
| overcoat | oet'u | 외투 |
| raincoat | piot | 비옷 |
| nightgown | chamot | 잠옷 |
| one-piece | wŏnp'isŭ | 원피스 |
| sweater | sŭwet'ŏ | 스웨터 |

| | | |
|---|---|---|
| skirt | sŭk'ŏt'ŭ | 스커트 |
| jumper | chamba | 잠바 |
| blouse | pŭllausŭ | 블라우스 |
| trousers | paji | 바지 |
| waistcoat | chokki | 조끼 |
| white shirt | waisyŏch'ŭ | 와이셔츠 |
| shirt | syŏch'ŭ | 셔츠 |
| hat | moja | 모자 |
| gloves | changgap | 장갑 |
| socks | yangmal | 양말 |
| stocking | kinyangmal | 긴양말 |
| muffler | mŏp'ŭllŏ | 머플러 |
| scarf | sŭk'ap'ŭ | 스카프 |
| handkerchief | sonsugŏn | 손수건 |
| button | tanch'u | 단추 |
| sleeve links | somaedanch'u | 소매단추 |
| rayon | reion | 레이온 |
| nylon | naillon | 나일론 |
| wool | mojik | 모직 |
| cotton | mumyŏng | 무명 |
| silk | myŏngju | 명주 |
| ring | panji | 반지 |
| necklace | mokkŏri | 목걸이 |
| bracelet | p'altchi | 팔찌 |
| earring | kwigŏri | 귀걸이 |

## VISITING
### 방 문(Pangmun)

| | | |
|---|---|---|
| call, visit | pangmun | 방문 |

| | | |
|---|---|---|
| introduction | sogae | 소개 |
| introduce | sogaehada | 소개하다 |
| caller, visitor | pangmunja(sonnim) | 방문자(손님) |
| guest | sonnim(naegaek) | 손님(내객) |
| unwelcome guest | pulch'ŏnggaek | 불청객 |
| master | chuin | 주인 |
| maid | hanyŏ | 하녀 |
| invitation | ch'odae | 초대 |
| party | moim | 모임 |
| warm greeting | hwandae | 환대 |
| cold reception | p'udaejŏp | 푸대접 |
| absence | pujae | 부재 |
| drop in | tŭllŭda | 들르다 |
| letter of introduction | sogaechang | 소개장 |
| calling card | myŏngham | 명함 |
| bell | ch'oinjong | 초인종 |

## TELEPHONE
### 전 화(Chŏnhwa)

| | | |
|---|---|---|
| public telephone | kongjung chŏnhwa | 공중 전화 |
| long distance call | shioe chŏnhwa | 시외 전화 |
| overseas service | kukche chŏnhwa | 국제 전화 |
| phone number | chŏnhwa pŏnho | 전화 번호 |
| telephone directory | chŏnhwa pŏnhobu | 전화 번호부 |
| telephone exchange | chŏnhwa kyohwan-guk | 전화 교환국 |
| telephone operator | chŏnhwa kyohwansu | 전화 교환수 |
| telephone message | t'onghwa | 통화 |
| dial | daiŏl | 다이얼 |

| | | |
|---|---|---|
| receiver | suhwagi | 수화기 |
| mouthpiece | songhwagi | 송화기 |
| wrong number | t'ŭllin pŏnho | 틀린 번호 |
| emergency call | pisang chŏnhwa | 비상 전화 |
| desk telephone | t'aksang chŏnhwa | 탁상 전화 |
| crossed wire | honsŏn | 혼선 |
| switchboard | kyohwan-gi | 교환기 |
| telephone charges | chŏnhwa yogŭm | 전화 요금 |
| extension | naesŏn | 내선 |
| telephone subscriber | chŏnhwa kaipcha | 전화 가입자 |

## POST OFFICE
### 우체국(Uch'eguk)

| | | |
|---|---|---|
| Central Post Office | chungang uch'eguk | 중앙 우체국 |
| International Parcel Post Office | kukche sop'o uch'eguk | 국제 소포 우체국 |
| mailbox | uch'et'ong | 우체통 |
| mailman | uch'ebu | 우체부 |
| air mail | hanggong up'yŏn | 항공 우편 |
| surface mail | sŏnbak up'yŏn | 선박 우편 |
| domestic post | kungnae up'yŏn | 국내 우편 |
| foreign post | oeguk up'yŏn | 외국 우편 |
| registered mail | tŭnggi up'yŏn | 등기 우편 |
| military post | kunsa up'yŏn | 군사 우편 |
| mail delivery | up'yŏn paedal | 우편 배달 |
| express delivery | soktal | 속달 |
| parcel post | sop'o | 소포 |
| letter | p'yŏnji | 편지 |
| stamp | up'yo | 우표 |

| | | |
|---|---|---|
| envelope | pongt'u | 봉투 |
| postal card | yŏpsŏ | 엽서 |
| picture post card | kŭrim yŏpsŏ | 그림 엽서 |
| telegram form | chŏnbo yongji | 전보 용지 |
| confidential | ch'injŏn | 친전 |
| tax | segŭm | 세금 |
| postage | up'yŏn yogŭm | 우편 요금 |
| postal order | up'yŏnhwan | 우편환 |
| revenue stamp | suip inji | 수입 인지 |
| commission | susuryo | 수수료 |
| printed matter | inswaemul | 인쇄물 |
| photo only | sajin chaejung | 사진 재중 |
| printed matter only | inswaemul chaejung | 인쇄물 재중 |
| address | chuso | 주소 |
| return address | palshinin chuso | 발신인 주소 |
| P. O. Box | sasŏham | 사서함 |

## MONEY AND BANK
### 돈과 은행(Ton-gwa Ŭnhaeng)

| | | |
|---|---|---|
| Bank of Korea | han-guk ŭnhaeng | 한국 은행 |
| The Commercial Bank of Korea | hanvit ŭnhaeng | 한빛 은행 |
| Korea Development Bank | han-guk sanŏp-ŭnhaeng | 한국 산업은행 |
| Foreign Exchange Bank | oehwan ŭnhaeng | 외환 은행 |
| Bank of Seoul | seoul ŭnhaeng | 서울 은행 |
| Korea Housing Bank | han-guk chut'aeg-ŭnhaeng | 한국 주택은행 |

| | | |
|---|---|---|
| Chohung bank | chohŭng ŭnhaeng | 조흥 은행 |
| Korea First Bank | cheil ŭnhaeng | 제일 은행 |
| Hanmi Bank | hanmi ŭnhaeng | 한미 은행 |
| money | ton(hwap'ye) | 돈(화폐) |
| note | chip'ye | 지폐 |
| cash | hyŏn-gŭm | 현금 |
| check | sup'yo | 수표 |
| checkbook | sup'yochang | 수표장 |
| bankbook | ŭnhaeng t'ongjang | 은행 통장 |
| bank deposit | yegŭm | 예금 |
| depositor | yegŭmja | 예금자 |
| dishonoured check | pudo sup'yo | 부도 수표 |
| current deposit | tangjwa yegŭm | 당좌 예금 |
| fixed deposit | chŏnggi yegŭm | 정기 예금 |
| deposit at notice | t'ongji yegŭm | 통지 예금 |
| trust fund | shint'ak chagŭm | 신탁 자금 |
| fiduciary loan | shinyong taebu | 신용 대부 |
| letter of credit | shinyongchang | 신용장 |
| capital | chabon | 자본 |
| loan | kongch'ae | 공채 |
| national debt | kukch'ae | 국채 |
| clearing house | ŏŭm kyohwanso | 어음 교환소 |
| I. O. U. | ch'ayong chŭngso | 차용 증서 |
| credit | ch'aekwŏn | 채권 |
| debt | ch'aemu | 채무 |
| bill of exchange | hwanŏŭm | 환어음 |
| rate of exchange | hwanyul | 환율 |
| loan rate | taebu iyul | 대부 이율 |
| remittance | songgŭm | 송금 |
| principal | wŏn-gŭm | 원금 |

| | | |
|---|---|---|
| interest | ija | 이자 |
| simple interest | talli | 단리 |
| compound interest | pongni | 복리 |
| securities | chŭngkwŏn | 증권 |

## DRUG AND HOSPITAL
### 약과 병원(Yakkwa Pyŏngwŏn)

| | | |
|---|---|---|
| drugstore | yakkuk | 약국 |
| druggist | yakchesa | 약제사 |
| prescription | ch'ŏbang | 처방 |
| medicine | yak | 약 |
| pill | hwanyak | 환약 |
| powder | karuyak | 가루약 |
| drug | maeyak | 매약 |
| tablet | chŏngje | 정제 |
| patent medicine | t'ŭk'ŏyak | 특허약 |
| prophylactic | yebangyak | 예방약 |
| styptic | chihyŏlyak | 지혈약 |
| disinfectant | sodongyak | 소독약 |
| intestinal medicine | wijangyak | 위장약 |
| laxative | sŏlsayak | 설사약 |
| binding medicine | sŏlsa kŭch'i-nŭn yak | 설사 그치는 약 |
| cold cure | kamgiyak | 감기약 |
| sleeping drug | sumyŏnje | 수면제 |
| febrifuge | haeyŏlche | 해열제 |
| tonic | kangjangje | 강장제 |
| emollient | wanhwaje | 완화제 |
| sedative | chinjŏngje | 진정제 |

| | | |
|---|---|---|
| antiseptic | pangbuje | 방부제 |
| deodorant | pangch'wije | 방취제 |
| cod-liver oil | kanyu | 간유 |
| boracic acid | pungsan | 붕산 |
| eye lotion | anyak | 안약 |
| opium | ap'yŏn | 아편 |
| iodine | oktojŏngki | 옥도정기 |
| compress | tchimjil | 찜질 |
| wound | sangch'ŏ | 상처 |
| bruise | t'abaksang | 타박상 |
| cut | pen sangch'ŏ | 벤 상처 |
| burn | hwasang | 화상 |
| chafing | ch'algwasang | 찰과상 |
| charge of medicine | yakkap | 약값 |
| hospital | pyŏngwŏn | 병원 |
| surgery | oekwa pyŏngwŏn | 외과 병원 |
| lunatic asylum | chŏngshin pyŏngwŏn | 정신 병원 |
| nose, ear and throat hospital | ibiinhukwa | 이비인후과 |
| gynaecological hospital | puinkwa pyŏngwŏn | 부인과 병원 |
| field hospital | yajŏn pyŏngwŏn | 야전 병원 |
| Red Cross Hospital | chŏkshipcha pyŏngwŏn | 적십자 병원 |
| doctor | ŭisa | 의사 |
| lady doctor | yŏŭisa | 여의사 |
| quack doctor | ŏngt'ŏri ŭisa | 엉터리 의사 |
| eye doctor | ankwa ŭisa | 안과 의사 |
| dentist | ch'ikwa ŭisa | 치과 의사 |
| assistant | chosu | 조수 |
| patient | hwanja | 환자 |

| | | |
|---|---|---|
| out-patient | oerae hwanja | 외래 환자 |
| inquiry office | chŏpsuch'ŏ | 접수처 |
| consultation ticket | chinch'alkwŏn | 진찰권 |
| consultation room | chinch'alshil | 진찰실 |
| sick ward | pyŏngshil | 병실 |
| operating room | susulshil | 수술실 |
| X-ray room | eksŭsŏnshil | 엑스선실 |
| cure | ch'iryo | 치료 |
| consulting fee | chinch'allyo | 진찰료 |
| medical examination | chinch'al | 진찰 |
| diagnosis | chindan | 진단 |
| call on a patient | wangjin kada. | 왕진 가다 |
| doctor's round of visit | hoejin | 회진 |
| first aid | ŭnggŭp ch'iryo | 응급 치료 |
| temperature | ch'eon | 체온 |
| thermometer | ch'eon-gye | 체온계 |
| ice pillow | ŏrŭm pegae | 얼음 베개 |
| ice bag | ŏrŭm chumŏni | 얼음 주머니 |
| ambulance | kugŭpch'a | 구급차 |
| disease | pyŏng | 병 |
| chronic | mansŏngŭi | 만성의 |
| acute | kŭpsŏngŭi | 급성의 |
| cold | kamgi | 감기 |
| influenza | yuhaengsŏng kamgi | 유행성 감기 |
| Chinese drug | hanyak | 한약 |
| headache | tut'ong | 두통 |
| toothache | ch'it'ong | 치통 |
| dyspepsia | sohwa pullyang | 소화 불량 |
| loose bowels | sŏlsa | 설사 |
| frostbite | tongsang | 동상 |

| | | |
|---|---|---|
| insommia | pulmyŏnchŭng | 불면증 |
| constipation | pyŏnbi | 변비 |
| appendicitis | maengjangyŏm | 맹장염 |
| tonsillitis | p'yŏndosŏnyŏm | 편도선염 |
| high blood pressure | kohyŏrap | 고혈압 |
| low blood pressure | chŏhyŏrap | 저혈압 |
| color blindness | saengmaeng | 색맹 |
| anemia | pinhyŏlchŭng | 빈혈증 |
| diabetes | tangnyopyŏng | 당뇨병 |
| heart trouble | shimjangpyŏng | 심장병 |
| kidney trouble | shinjangpyŏng | 신장병 |
| epidemic | chŏnyŏmpyŏng | 전염병 |
| dysentery | ijil | 이질 |
| consumption | p'yepyŏng | 폐병 |
| tuberculosis | kyŏrhaek | 결핵 |
| smallpox | ch'ŏnyŏndu | 천연두 |
| measles | hongyŏk | 홍역 |
| cholera | k'ollera | 콜레라 |
| diphtheria | tip'ŭt'eria | 디프테리아 |
| scarlet fever | sŏnghongyŏl | 성홍열 |
| whooping cough | paegirhae | 백일해 |
| malaria | hakchil | 학질 |
| pest | p'esŭt'ŭ | 페스트 |
| typhoid fever | changt'ip'usŭ | 장티푸스 |
| venereal disease | sŏngpyŏng | 성병 |
| syphilis | maedok | 매독 |
| gonorrhoea | imjil | 임질 |
| cancer | am | 암 |

## LANGUAGE
## 언 어(Ŏnŏ)

| | | |
|---|---|---|
| living language | hyŏndaeŏ | 현대어 |
| dead language | saŏ | 사어 |
| spoken language | kuŏ | 구어 |
| written language | munŏ | 문어 |
| universal language | segyeŏ | 세계어 |
| mother tongue | mogugŏ | 모국어 |
| diplomatic language | oegyo yongŏ | 외교 용어 |
| commercial language | sangŏp yongŏ | 상업 용어 |
| Korean | Han-gugŏ | 한국어 |
| Chinese | Chunggugŏ | 중국어 |
| German | Togirŏ | 독일어 |
| English | Yŏngŏ | 영어 |
| French | P'ŭrangsŭŏ | 프랑스어 |
| Japanese | Ilbonŏ | 일본어 |
| Italian | It'alliaŏ | 이탈리아어 |
| Latin | Latinŏ | 라틴어 |
| Greek | Kŭrisŭŏ | 그리스어 |
| Spanish | Sŭp'einŏ | 스페인어 |
| Esperanto | Esŭp'erant'oŏ | 에스페란토어 |
| Standard language | p'yojunŏ | 표준어 |
| dialect | sat'uri | 사투리 |
| abbreviation | yagŏ | 약어 |
| idiom | kwanyongŏ | 관용어 |
| everyday expression | sangyongŏ | 상용어 |
| phrase | sugŏ | 숙어 |
| slang | sogŏ | 속어 |

| | | |
|---|---|---|
| synonym | tongŭiŏ | 동의어 |
| antonym | panŭiŏ | 반의어 |
| diction | ŏpŏp | 어법 |
| grammar | munpŏp | 문법 |
| elocution | palsŏngpŏp | 발성법 |
| accentuation | aeksent'ŭpŏp | 액센트법 |
| pronunciation | parŭm | 발음 |
| vocabulary | ŏhwi | 어휘 |

## EDUCATION
교육(Kyoyuk)

| | | |
|---|---|---|
| compulsory education | ŭimu kyoyuk | 의무 교육 |
| home education | kajŏng kyoyuk | 가정 교육 |
| practical education | shirŏp kyoyuk | 실업 교육 |
| vocational education | chigŏp kyoyuk | 직업 교육 |
| kindergarten | yuch'iwŏn | 유치원 |
| elementary school | ch'odŭng hakkyo | 초등 학교 |
| middle school | chunghakkyo | 중학교 |
| high school | kodŭng hakkyo | 고등 학교 |
| technical high school | kongŏp kodŭng hakkyo | 공업 고등 학교 |
| commercial high school | sangŏp kodŭng hakkyo | 상업 고등 학교 |
| junior college | chŏnmun taehak | 전문 대학 |
| teacher's college | kyoyuk taehak | 교육 대학 |
| university | chonghap taehak | 종합 대학 |
| state college | kungnip taehak | 국립 대학 |
| private college | sarip taehak | 사립 대학 |
| electrical engineering | chŏn-gi konghak | 전기 공학 |

| | | |
|---|---|---|
| mechanical engineering | kigye konghak | 기계 공학 |
| coeducation | namnyŏ konghak | 남녀 공학 |
| literature | munhak | 문학 |
| natural science | chayŏn kwahak | 자연 과학 |
| social science | sahoe kwahak | 사회 과학 |
| medicine | ŭihak | 의학 |
| dentistry | ch'itkwa ŭihak | 치과 의학 |
| agriculture | nonghak | 농학 |
| philosophy | ch'ŏrhak | 철학 |
| logic | nollihak | 논리학 |
| sociology | sahoehak | 사회학 |
| biology | saengmurhak | 생물학 |
| physical geography | chayŏn chirihak | 자연 지리학 |
| astronomy | ch'ŏnmunhak | 천문학 |
| psychology | shimnihak | 심리학 |
| economics | kyŏngjehak | 경제학 |
| civil engineering | t'omok konghak | 토목 공학 |
| history | yŏksa | 역사 |
| geography | chiri | 지리 |
| mathematics | suhak | 수학 |
| industrial engineering | sanŏp kisul | 산업 기술 |
| political science | chŏngch'ihak | 정치학 |
| law | pŏp'ak | 법학 |
| chemistry | hwahak | 화학 |
| physics | mullihak | 물리학 |
| geology | chijirhak | 지질학 |
| shorthand | sokki | 속기 |
| bookkeeping | pugi | 부기 |
| business administration | kyŏngyŏnghak | 경영학 |

| | | |
|---|---|---|
| physical education | ch'eyuk | 체육 |
| optional subject | sŏnt'aek kwamok | 선택 과목 |
| compulsory subject | p'ilsu kwamok | 필수 과목 |
| director | kyojang | 교장(고등 학교) |
| principal | kyojang | 교장 |
| headmaster | kyojang | 교장 |
| teacher | kyosa | 교사 |
| professor | kyosu | 교수 |
| student | haksaeng | 학생 |
| doctor | paksa | 박사 |
| honor student | udŭngsaeng | 우등생 |
| scholarship student | changhaksaeng | 장학생 |
| dormitory | kisuksa | 기숙사 |
| campus | kyojŏng | 교정 |
| alma mater | mogyo | 모교 |
| commencement | chorŏpshik | 졸업식 |
| thesis | chorŏp nonmun | 졸업 논문 |
| examination | shihŏm | 시험 |
| tuition | suŏmnyo | 수업료 |
| part-time job | arŭbait'ŭ | 아르바이트 |
| cheating | k'ŏning | 커닝 |

## SPORTS
## 운 동(Undong)

| | | |
|---|---|---|
| ground | undongjang | 운동장 |
| athletic meeting | undonghoe | 운동회 |
| gymnastics | ch'ejo | 체조 |
| tournament | shihap | 시합 |
| marathon | marat'on | 마라톤 |

| | | |
|---|---|---|
| running high jump | nop'ittwigi | 높이뛰기 |
| running broad jump | nŏlbittwigi | 넓이뛰기 |
| track and field events | yuksang kyŏnggi | 육상 경기 |
| swimming race | suyŏng kyŏnggi | 수영 경기 |
| race | kyŏngju | 경주 |
| boat race | pot'ŭ kyŏngju | 보트 경주 |
| yacht race | yot'ŭ kyŏngju | 요트 경주 |
| bicycle race | chajọn-gŏ kyŏngju | 자전거 경주 |
| discus | wŏnban dŏnjigi | 원반던지기 |
| shotput | p'ohwan dŏnjigi | 포환던지기 |
| fencing | kŏmsul | 검술 |
| basketball | nonggu | 농구 |
| association football | ch'ukku | 축구 |
| American football | mishik ch'ukku | 미식 축구 |
| rugby | rŏkpi | 럭비 |
| baseball | yagu | 야구 |
| tennis | chŏnggu | 정구 |
| volleyball | paegu | 배구 |
| handball | haendŭbol | 핸드볼 |
| pingpong | t'akku | 탁구 |
| billiard | tanggu | 당구 |
| skiing | sŭk'iing | 스키잉 |
| hockey | hak'i | 하키 |
| ice hocky | aisŭ hak'i | 아이스 하키 |
| field hocky | pildŭ hak'i | 필드 하키 |
| skating | sŭk'eit'ing | 스케이팅 |
| figure skating | p'igyŏ sŭk'eit'ing | 피겨 스케이팅 |
| bowling | polling | 볼링 |
| swimming | suyŏng | 수영 |

| | | |
|---|---|---|
| judo | yudo | 유도 |
| t'aekwŏndo | t'aekwŏndo | 태권도 |
| wrestling | resŭlling | 레슬링 |
| weight-lifting | yŏkki | 역기 |
| boxing | kwŏnt'u | 권투 |
| horse riding | sŭngma | 승마 |
| horse racing | kyŏngma | 경마 |
| camping | k'aemp'ing | 캠핑 |
| mountain climbing | tŭngsan | 등산 |
| mountaineer | tŭngsan-ga | 등산가 |
| golf | kolp'ŭ | 골프 |
| golf club | kolp'ŭch'ae (kolp'ŭ k'ŭllŏp) | 골프채 (골프 클럽) |
| caddie | kong chumnŭn saram | 공 줍는 사람 |
| goal | kyŏlsŭng | 결승 |
| skipping | chullŏmki | 줄넘기 |
| club | konbong | 곤봉 |

## OCCUPATIONS
### 직 업(Chigŏp)

| | | |
|---|---|---|
| scholar | hakcha | 학자 |
| poet | shiin | 시인 |
| artist | misulga(hwaga) | 미술가(화가) |
| penman | sŏdoga | 서도가 |
| writer | chakka | 작가 |
| translator | pŏnyŏkka | 번역가 |
| proofreader | kyojŏngga | 교정가 |
| critic | pip'yŏngga | 비평가 |
| philosopher | ch'ŏrhakcha | 철학자 |

| | | |
|---|---|---|
| historian | yŏksaga | 역사가 |
| zoologist | tongmulhakcha | 동물학자 |
| botanist | shingmulhakcha | 식물학자 |
| journalist | shinmun kija | 신문 기자 |
| interpreter | t'ongyŏkcha | 통역자 |
| civil engineer | t'omok kisa | 토목 기사 |
| engineer | kigye kisa | 기계 기사 |
| surveyor | ch'ŭngnyangga | 측량가 |
| physician | naekwa ŭisa | 내과 의사 |
| surgeon | oekwa ŭisa | 외과 의사 |
| lawyer | pyŏnhosa | 변호사 |
| nurse | kanhowŏn | 간호원 |
| shoemaker | chehwagong | 제화공 |
| jeweller | posŏksang | 보석상 |
| watchmaker | shigyesang | 시계상 |
| glazier | yurisang | 유리상 |
| carpenter | moksu | 목수 |
| printer | inswaeŏpcha | 인쇄업자 |
| bookbinder | chebonŏpcha | 제본업자 |
| shipbuilder | chosŏnŏpcha | 조선업자 |
| hawker | haengsangin | 행상인 |
| merchant | sangin | 상인 |
| civil servant | kongmuwŏn | 공무원 |
| office man | hoesawŏn | 회사원 |
| banker | ŭnhaengga | 은행가 |
| clerk | samuwŏn | 사무원 |
| barber | ibalsa | 이발사 |
| photographer | sajinsa | 사진사 |
| tailor | chaebongsa | 재봉사 |
| farmer | nongbu | 농부 |

| | | |
|---|---|---|
| fisher | ŏbu | 어부 |
| miner | kwangbu | 광부 |

## BOOKS
책(Ch'aek)

| | | |
|---|---|---|
| author | chakka | 작가 |
| authoress | yŏryu chakka | 여류 작가 |
| publisher | ch'ulp'anŏpcha | 출판업자 |
| novelist | sosŏlga | 소설가 |
| poet | shiin | 시인 |
| great reader | toksŏga | 독서가 |
| bookworm | toksŏgwang | 독서광 |
| coauthor | kongjŏja | 공저자 |
| literature | munhak | 문학 |
| pure literature | sunsu munhak | 순수 문학 |
| literary magazine | munhak chapchi | 문학 잡지 |
| classic | kojŏn | 고전 |
| biography | chŏn-gi | 전기 |
| autobiography | chasŏjŏn | 자서전 |
| directory | inmyŏngnok | 인명록 |
| anthology | myŏngshisŏnjip | 명시선집 |
| poetical works | shijip | 시집 |
| dictionary | sajŏn | 사전 |
| encyclopedia | paekkwasajŏn | 백과사전 |
| textbook | kyogwasŏ | 교과서 |
| reference book | ch'amgosŏ | 참고서 |
| conversation book | hoehwa ch'aek | 회화 책 |
| guidebook | annaesŏ | 안내서 |
| comic book | manhwach'aek | 만화책 |

| | | |
|---|---|---|
| fairy tale | tonghwa | 동화 |
| Bible | sŏngsŏ | 성서 |
| diary | ilgi | 일기 |
| travel book | yŏhaenggi | 여행기 |
| poetry | shi | 시 |
| prose | sanmun | 산문 |
| essay | sup'il | 수필 |
| short story | tanp'yŏn | 단편 |
| medium-length story | chungp'yŏn sosŏl | 중편 소설 |
| long novel | changp'yŏn sosŏl | 장편 소설 |
| love story | yŏnae sosŏl | 연애 소설 |
| science fiction | kwahak sosŏl | 과학 소설 |
| historical novel | yŏksa sosŏl | 역사 소설 |
| detective story | t'amjŏng sosŏl | 탐정 소설 |
| whodunit | ch'uri sosŏl | 추리 소설 |
| mystery story | koegi sosŏl | 괴기 소설 |
| magazine | chapchi | 잡지 |
| periodicals | chŏnggiganhaengmul | 정기 간행물 |
| weekly | chugan | 주간 |
| monthly | wŏlgan | 월간 |
| quarterly | kyegan | 계간 |
| revised edition | kaejŏngp'an | 개정판 |
| enlarged edition | chŭngbop'an | 증보판 |
| preface | sŏmun | 서문 |
| prologue | sŏron | 서론 |
| epilogue | kyŏllon | 결론 |
| main subject | pollon | 본론 |
| nonfiction | shirhwa | 실화 |
| fiction | hŏgu | 허구 |
| impression | insang | 인상 |

## NEWSPAPER, RADIO, TV
## 신문, 라디오, 텔레비전
## (Shinmun, Radio, T'ellebijŏn)

| | | |
|---|---|---|
| newspaper | shinmun | 신문 |
| morning edition | chogan | 조간 |
| evening edition | sŏkkan | 석간 |
| daily | ilgan shinmun | 일간 신문 |
| weekly | chugan shinmun | 주간 신문 |
| yellow sheet | chŏsok shinmun | 저속 신문 |
| English edition | yŏngcha shinmun | 영자 신문 |
| extra | hooe | 호외 |
| newspaper office | shinmunsa | 신문사 |
| war correspondent | chonggun kija | 종군 기자 |
| correspondent | t'ongshinwŏn | 통신원 |
| reporter | t'ambangwŏn | 탐방원 |
| chief editor | p'yŏnjipchang | 편집장 |
| editor | p'yŏnjibwŏn | 편집원 |
| news man(boy) | shinmun paedarwŏn | 신문 배달원 |
| news stand | shinmun maejŏm | 신문 매점 |
| news board | keship'an | 게시판 |
| editor-in-chief | chup'il | 주필 |
| discourse | nonsŏl | 논설 |
| editorial | sasŏl | 사설 |
| hot news | saesoshik | 새소식 |
| topic | hwaje | 화제 |
| current topics | onŭrŭi hwaje | 오늘의 화제 |
| fashion topics | yuhaeng hwaje | 유행 화제 |
| article | kisa | 기사 |

| | | |
|---|---|---|
| big news | k'ŭn kisa | 큰 기사 |
| exclusive story | tokchŏm kisa | 독점 기사 |
| news flash | chigŭppo | 지급보 |
| libelous report | chungsangjŏk kisa | 중상적 기사 |
| political news | chŏngch'i nyusŭ | 정치 뉴스 |
| headline | chemok | 제목 |
| literary critic | munyep'yŏng | 문예평 |
| music review | ŭmakp'yŏng | 음악평 |
| book review | sŏp'yŏng | 서평 |
| readers column | tokchanan | 독자난 |
| general news column | chapsoshingnan | 잡소식난 |
| ad column | kwanggonan | 광고난 |
| advertisement | kwanggo | 광고 |
| classified ad | kuin kwanggo | 구인 광고 |
| comic | manhwa | 만화 |
| cut | sap'wa | 삽화 |
| government organ | chŏngbu kigwanji | 정부 기관지 |
| subscription | kudok | 구독 |
| circulation | parhaeng pusu | 발행 부수 |
| news value | podo kach'i | 보도 가치 |
| misprint | oshik | 오식 |
| freedom of the press | ch'ulp'an podoŭi chayu | 출판 보도의 자유 |
| press ban | parhaeng chŏngji | 발행 정지 |
| supress a story | kisa palp'yorŭl kŭmjihada | 기사 발표를 금지하다 |
| censor | kŏmyŏrhada | 검열하다 |
| broadcasting station | pangsongguk | 방송국 |
| radio studio | pangsongshil | 방송실 |
| radio network | pangsongmang | 방송망 |

| | | |
|---|---|---|
| public service broadcasting | konggong pangsong | 공공 방송 |
| commercial broadcasting | min-gan pangsong | 민간 방송 |
| commercial program | sangŏp pangsong | 상업 방송 |
| running commentary | shirhwang pangsong | 실황 방송 |
| rebroadcast | chunggye pangsong | 중계 방송 |
| television broadcast | t'elebijŏn pangsong | 텔레비전 방송 |
| broadcasting program | pangsong sunsŏ | 방송 순서 |
| radio drama | pangsonggŭk | 방송극 |
| radio forum | radio t'oronhoe | 라디오 토론회 |
| radio editorial | radio shisa haesŏl | 라디오 시사 해설 |
| weather reports | ilgi yebo | 일기 예보 |
| radio concert | pangsong ŭmak | 방송 음악 |
| radio quiz | radio k'wijŭ | 라디오 퀴즈 |
| antenna | ant'ena | 안테나 |
| loudspeaker | hwaksŏnggi | 확성기 |
| portable microphone | hyudaeyong maik'ŭrop'on | 휴대용 마이크로폰 |
| home receiver | kajŏngyong susanggi | 가정용 수상기 |
| transmitter | songp'agi | 송파기 |
| video signal | t'elebijŏn shinho | 텔레비전 신호 |
| police radio | kyŏngch'al mujŏn | 경찰 무전 |
| patrol car | sunhoech'a | 순회차 |
| announcer | anaunsŏ | 아나운서 |
| radio listener | radio ch'ŏngch'wija | 라디오 청취자 |

# HOBBY
## 취 미(Ch'wimi)

| | | |
|---|---|---|
| angler | nakshikkun | 낚시꾼 |
| off shore fishing | pada nakshijil | 바다 낚시질 |
| river fishing | kang nakshijil | 강 낚시질 |
| fishing tackle | nakshi kigu | 낚시 기구 |
| hook | nakshi | 낚시 |
| fishing rod | nakshittae | 낚싯대 |
| float | nakshitchi | 낚시찌 |
| bait | nakshitpap(mikki) | 낚싯밥(미끼) |
| fishing place | .nakshit'ŏ | 낚시터 |
| fishing ground | ŏjang | 어장 |
| riverside | kangka | 강가 |
| seashore | padatka | 바닷가 |
| fishing boat | kogijabi pae | 고기잡이 배 |
| hunting | sanyang | 사냥 |
| hunter | sanyangkkŭn | 사냥꾼 |
| hunting licence | suryŏp myŏnhŏ | 수렵 면허 |
| hunting ground | sanyangt'ŏ | 사냥터 |
| hound | sanyangkae | 사냥개 |
| crackshot | myŏngp'osu | 명포수 |
| gun | ch'ong | 총 |
| shotgun | yŏpch'ong | 엽총 |
| air gun | konggich'ong | 공기총 |
| automatic gun | chadongch'ong | 자동총 |
| cartridge | yakp'o | 약포 |
| bore | ch'ongkumŏng | 총구멍 |
| shot | t'anhwan | 탄환 |

| | | |
|---|---|---|
| camera | sajinki | 사진기 |
| photo artist | sajin-ga | 사진가 |
| camera bug | sajin-gwang | 사진광 |
| photographic contest | sajin ch'waryŏng taehoe | 사진 촬영 대회 |
| color film | k'ŏllŏ p'illŭm | 컬러 필름 |
| black and white film | hŭkpaek p'illŭm | 흑백 필름 |
| development | hyŏnsang | 현상 |
| printing | inhwa | 인화 |
| enlargement | hwaktae | 확대 |
| folk song | minyo | 민요 |
| song | norae | 노래 |
| popular song | yuhaengga | 유행가 |
| lullaby | chajangga | 자장가 |
| national anthem | kukka | 국가 |
| classical music | kojŏn ŭmak | 고전 음악 |
| chamber music | shillaeak | 실내악 |
| nocturne | yasanggok | 야상곡 |
| fantasia | hwansanggok | 환상곡 |
| rhapsody | kwangsanggok | 광상곡 |
| concert | yŏnjuhoe | 연주회 |
| charity concert | chasŏn yŏnjuhoe | 자선 연주회 |
| recital | tokchuhoe | 독주회 |
| composer | chakkokka | 작곡가 |
| conductor | chihwija | 지휘자 |
| vocalist | sŏngakka | 성악가 |
| chorus | hapch'angdae | 합창대 |
| solo | tokchu | 독주 |
| accompaniment | panju | 반주 |
| brass band | aktae | 악대 |

| | | |
|---|---|---|
| trumpet | nap'al | 나팔 |
| gardening | wŏnye | 원예 |
| horticulture | wŏnyesul | 원예술 |
| floriculture | hwach'o chaebae | 화초 재배 |
| flower | kkot | 꽃 |
| flower arrangement | kkotkkoji | 꽃꽂이 |
| artificial flower | chohwa | 조화 |
| pot-planting | punjae | 분재 |
| flowerpot | hwabun | 화분 |
| dance | muyong(ch'um) | 무용(춤) |
| stamp collection | up'yo sujip | 우표 수집 |
| stamp collector | up'yo sujipka | 우표 수집가 |

## MOVIES AND PLAYS
## 영화와 연극(Yŏnghwawa Yŏn-gŭk)

| | | |
|---|---|---|
| silent movie | musŏng yŏnghwa | 무성 영화 |
| 3-D picture | ipch'e yŏnghwa | 입체 영화 |
| black and white film | hŭkpaek yŏnghwa | 흑백 영화 |
| technicolor film | ch'ŏnyŏnsaek yŏnghwa | 천연색 영화 |
| drama movie | kŭngyŏnghwa | 극영화 |
| newsreel | nyusŭ yŏnghwa | 뉴우스 영화 |
| literary film | munye yŏnghwa | 문예 영화 |
| musical film | ŭmak yŏnghwa | 음악 영화 |
| documentary film | kirok yŏnghwa | 기록 영화 |
| culture film | munhwa yŏnghwa | 문화 영화 |
| educational film | kyoyuk yŏnghwa | 교육 영화 |
| animated cartoon | manhwa yŏnghwa | 만화 영화 |
| producer | yŏnghwa chejakcha | 영화 제작자 |

| | | |
|---|---|---|
| director | kamdok | 감독 |
| star | chuyŏn | 주연 |
| film actor | yŏnghwa paeu | 영화 배우 |
| film actress | yŏnghwa yŏbaeu | 영화 여배우 |
| juvenile actor | ayŏk paeu | 아역 배우 |
| character actor | sŏngkyŏk paeu | 성격 배우 |
| movie fan | yŏnghwa p'aen | 영화 팬 |
| audience | kwan-gaek | 관객 |
| cameraman | ch'waryŏng kisa | 촬영 기사 |
| studio | ch'waryŏngjang | 촬영장 |
| movie house | yŏnghwagwan | 영화관 |
| play theater | kŭkchang | 극장 |
| double role | irin iyok | 일인 이역 |
| title | chamak | 자막 |
| scenario | shinario | 시나리오 |
| admission | ipchangnyo | 입장료 |
| drama | hŭigok | 희곡 |
| comedy | hŭigŭk | 희극 |
| tragedy | pigŭk | 비극 |
| satire | p'ungjagŭk | 풍자극 |
| pantomime | muŏn-gŭk | 무언극 |
| playwright | kukchakka | 극작가 |
| producer | yŏnch'ulga | 연출가 |
| actor | paeu | 배우 |
| actress | yŏbaeu | 여배우 |
| part | yŏk | 역 |
| dialogue | taehwa | 대화 |
| scenary | paegyŏng | 배경 |
| stage | mudae | 무대 |
| auditorium | kwallamsŏk | 관람석 |

| | | |
|---|---|---|
| scene | changmyŏn | 장면 |
| curtain | mak | 막 |
| presentation | sangyŏn | 상연 |
| intermission | hyuge shigan | 휴게 시간 |
| lounge | hyugeshil | 휴게실 |
| ticket office | maep'yoso | 매표소 |
| advance tickets | yemaekwŏn | 예매권 |
| full house | manwŏn | 만원 |

## ANIMALS
동물(Tongmul)

| | | |
|---|---|---|
| beast | chimsŭng | 짐승 |
| wild animals | yasu | 야수 |
| lion | saja | 사자 |
| lioness | amsaja | 암사자 |
| tiger | horangi | 호랑이 |
| tigeress | amhorangi | 암호랑이 |
| leopard | p'yobŏm | 표범 |
| wolf | nŭktae | 늑대 |
| fox | yŏu | 여우 |
| bear | kom | 곰 |
| elephant | k'okkiri | 코끼리 |
| wild boar | santwaeji | 산돼지 |
| camel | nakt'a | 낙타 |
| wildcat | salk'waengi | 살쾡이 |
| monkey | wŏnsungi | 원숭이 |
| deer | sasŭm (noru) | 사슴(노루) |
| snake | paem | 뱀 |
| horse | mal | 말 |

| | | |
|---|---|---|
| bull | hwangso | 황소 |
| cow | amso | 암소 |
| pig | twaeji | 돼지 |
| dog | kae | 개 |
| cat | koyangi | 고양이 |
| sheep | yang | 양 |
| hare | sant'okki | 산토끼 |
| rabbit | chipt'okki | 집토끼 |
| mouse | saengjwi | 생쥐 |
| rat | chwi | 쥐 |
| pigeon | pidulgi | 비둘기 |
| eagle | toksuri | 독수리 |
| pheasant | kkwŏng | 꿩 |
| turkey | ch'ilmyŏnjo | 칠면조 |
| swallow | chebi | 제비 |
| sparrow | ch'amsae | 참새 |
| crow | kkamagwi | 까마귀 |
| duck | ori | 오리 |
| quail | mech'uragi | 메추라기 |
| snipe | toyosae | 도요새 |
| wild goose | kirŏgi | 기러기 |
| wild duck | tŭrori | 들오리 |
| hawk | mae | 매 |
| water-fowl | mulsae | 물새 |
| goose | kŏwi | 거위 |
| migratory bird | ch'ŏlsae | 철새 |
| bird | sae | 새 |
| insect | konch'ung | 곤충 |
| mosquito | mogi | 모기 |
| silkworm | nue | 누에 |

| | | |
|---|---|---|
| fly | p'ari | 파리 |
| butterfly | nabi | 나비 |
| ant | kaemi | 개미 |
| firefly | kaettongbŏlle | 개똥벌레 |
| cicada | maemi | 매미 |
| seal | padap'yobŏm | 바다표범 |
| whale | korae | 고래 |
| shark | sangŏ | 상어 |
| catfish | megi | 메기 |
| halibut, flatfish | kajami | 가자미 |
| perch | nongŏdŭngsok | 농어등속 |
| plaice | nŏpch'i | 넙치 |
| sea bream | tomi | 도미 |
| mullet | sungŏ | 숭어 |
| globefish | pogŏ | 복어 |
| cod | taegu | 대구 |
| haddock | taegudŭngsok | 대구등속 |
| stingray | kaori | 가오리 |
| mackerel | kodungŏ | 고등어 |
| herring | ch'ŏngŏ | 청어 |
| salmon | yŏnŏ | 연어 |
| sardine | chŏngŏri | 정어리 |
| yellowtail | pangŏ | 방어 |
| goby | mangdungi | 망둥이 |
| squid | ojingŏ | 오징어 |
| cuttlefish | ojingŏdŭngsok | 오징어등속 |
| carp | ingŏ | 잉어 |
| trout | songŏ | 송어 |
| smelt | pingŏ | 빙어 |
| gible | pungŏ | 붕어 |

| | | |
|---|---|---|
| eel | paemjangŏ | 뱀장어 |
| lobster | wangsaeu | 왕새우 |
| shrimp | saeu | 새우 |
| loach | mikkuraji | 미꾸라지 |
| crab | ke | 게 |
| sea-cucumber | haesam | 해삼 |
| crawfish | kajae | 가재 |
| shellfish | chogae | 조개 |
| oyster | kul | 굴 |
| goldfish | kŭmbungŏ | 금붕어 |

## POLITICS, ADMINISTRATION
정치, 행정(Chŏngch'i, Haengjŏng)

| | | |
|---|---|---|
| the state | kukka | 국가 |
| people | kungmin | 국민 |
| citizen | shimin | 시민 |
| head of the state | kukkawŏnsu | 국가원수 |
| president | taet'ongnyŏng | 대통령 |
| vice-president | put'ongnyŏng | 부통령 |
| goverment | chŏngbu | 정부 |
| Administration | haengjŏngbu | 행정부 |
| federal government | yŏnbang chŏngbu | 연방 정부 |
| Ministry of Finance and Economy | chaejŏngkyungjebu | 재정경제부 |
| Ministry of Information Communications | chŏngbot'ongsinbu | 정보통신부 |
| Ministry of Commerce Industry and Energy | sanŭpjawŏnbu | 산업자원부 |

| | | |
|---|---|---|
| Ministry of Foreign Affairs and Trade | oekyot'ongsangbu | 외교통상부 |
| Ministry of Government Administration and Home affairs | hangjŏngjachibu | 행정자치부 |
| Ministry of Agriculture and Forestry | nongrimbu | 농림부 |
| Ministry of Maritime Affairs and Fisheries | haeyangsusanbu | 해양수산부 |
| Ministry of Construction and Transport | kŏnsŏlkyot'ongbu | 건설교통부 |
| Ministry of Health and Welfare | pogŏnbokjibu | 보건복지부 |
| Ministry of Culture and Tourism | munhwagwangwangbu | 문화관광부 |
| Ministry of Labor | nodongbu | 노동부 |
| Executive branch | haengjŏngbu | 행정부 |
| Legislative branch | ippŏppu | 입법부 |
| Judiciary branch | sabŏppu | 사법부 |
| | | |
| Prime Minister | kungmu Ch'ongni | 국무총리 |
| Secretary of Defence | kukpangbu changgwan | 국방부장관 |
| Secretary of Interior | naemubu changgwan | 내무부장관 |
| Secretary of Finance and Economy | chaejŏngkyongjepu changgwan | 재정경제부장관 |
| Secretary of Justice | pŏmmubu changgwan | 법무부 장관 |
| Secretary of Unification | t'ongilbu changgwan | 통일부 장관 |
| Secretary of Health and Welfare | Pogonbokjibu Changgwan | 보건복지부장관 |

| | | |
|---|---|---|
| Attorney general | kŏmch'alch'ongjang | 검찰총장 |
| Provincial Governor | tojisa | 도지사 |
| minister | changgwan, kongsa | 장관, 공사 |
| cabinet | naegak | 내각 |
| cabinet meeting | kagŭi | 각의 |
| congress | kuk'oe | 국회 |
| committee | wiwŏnhoe | 위원회 |
| sub-committee | punkwa wiwŏnhoe | 분과 위원회 |
| vote | p'yogyŏl, ŭigyŏl | 표결, 의결 |
| ratification | pijun | 비준 |
| budget | yesan | 예산 |
| fiscal year | hoegye yŏndo | 회계 연도 |
| receipt | seip | 세입 |
| expenditure | sech'ul | 세출 |
| Chief Justice | taebŏbwŏnjang | 대법원장 |
| justice | pŏpkwan | 법관 |
| jury | paeshimwŏn | 배심원 |
| supreme court | taebŏbwŏn | 대법원 |
| ambassador | taesa | 대사 |
| ambassadress | taesa puin, yŏdaesa | 대사 부인, 여대사 |
| consul | yŏngsa | 영사 |
| acting consul | taeri yŏngsa | 대리 영사 |
| diplomat | oegyogwan | 외교관 |
| embassy | taesagwan | 대사관 |
| legation | kongsagwan | 공사관 |
| consulate | yŏngsagwan | 영사관 |
| credential | shinimchang | 신임장 |
| recognition | sŭngin | 승인 |
| session | hoegi | 회기 |

| | | |
|---|---|---|
| veto | kŏbukwŏn | 거부권 |
| Republican Party | konghwadang | 공화당 |
| Democratic Party | minjudang | 민주당 |
| democracy | minjujuŭi | 민주주의 |
| freedom | chayu | 자유 |
| general election | ch'ongsŏn-gŏ | 총선거 |
| ballot | t'up'yo | 투표 |
| election campaign | sŏn-gŏ yuse | 선거 유세 |
| candidate | huboja | 후보자 |
| economic development | kyŏngje kaebal | 경제 개발 |
| foreign aid | taeoe wŏnjo | 대외 원조 |
| tax | segŭm | 세금 |
| treasury | kukko | 국고 |
| national debt | kukch'ae | 국채 |
| public debt | kongch'ae | 공채 |
| fine | kwaryo | 과료 |
| Integrated Government Building | chonghap ch'ŏngsa | 종합 청사 |
| Chamber of Commerce and Industry | sanggong hoeŭiso | 상공 회의소 |
| local self-government | chibang chach'i | 지방 자치 |
| provincial office | toch'ŏng | 도청 |
| city hall | shich'ŏng | 시청 |
| district office | kunch'ŏng | 군청 |
| village office | tonghoe | 동회 |
| police station | kyŏngch'alsŏ | 경찰서 |
| policebox | p'ach'ulso | 파출소 |
| customhouse | segwan | 세관 |
| mayor | shijang | 시장 |
| magistrate | kunsu | 군수 |

| | | |
|---|---|---|
| detective | hyŏngsa | 형사 |
| underdeveloped country | chŏgaebalguk | 저개발국 |
| ally | tongmaengguk | 동맹국 |
| neutral nation | chungnipkuk | 중립국 |
| peace offensive | p'yŏnghwa kongse | 평화 공세 |
| peak conference | chŏngsang hoedam | 정상 회담 |
| press interview | Kija hoegyŏn | 기자 회견 |
| anti-communist | pan-gong | 반공 |
| revolution | hyŏngmyŏng | 혁명 |
| martial law | kyeŏmnyŏng | 계엄령 |

## MILITARY

군사 용어 (Kunsa Yongo)

| | | |
|---|---|---|
| General of Army | wŏnsu | 원수 |
| General | taejang | 대장 |
| Lieutenant General | chungjang | 중장 |
| Major General | sojang | 소장 |
| Brigadier General | chunjang | 준장 |
| Colonel | taeryŏng | 대령 |
| Lieutenant Colonel | chungnyŏng | 중령 |
| Major | soryŏng | 소령 |
| Captain | taewi | 대위 |
| First Lieutenant | chungwi | 중위 |
| Second Lieutenant | sowi | 소위 |
| Warrant Officer | chunwi | 준위 |
| Command Sergeant Major | wŏnsa | 원사 |
| Master Sergeant | sangsa | 상사 |
| Sergeant, 1st class | chungsa | 중사 |

| | | |
|---|---|---|
| Staff Sergeant | hasa | 하사 |
| Sergeant | pyŏngjang | 병장 |
| Corporal | sangbyŏng | 상병 |
| Private, 1st class | iltŭngbyŏng | 1등병 |
| Private | idŭngbyŏng | 2등병 |
| Recruit | shinbyŏng | 신병 |
| Chief Petty Officer | pyŏngjojang | 병조장 |
| Petty Officer, 1st class | iltŭng pyŏngjo | 1등 병조 |
| Petty Officer, 2nd class | idŭng pyŏngjo | 2등 병조 |
| Petty Officer, 3rd class | samdŭng pyŏngjo | 3등 병조 |
| Seaman, 1st class | iltŭng sŭbyŏng | 1등 수병 |
| Seaman, 2nd class | idŭng subyŏng | 2등 수병 |
| Apprentice Seaman | s´ dŭng subyŏng | 3등 수병 |
| Chairman of the Joint Chiefs Staff | yonhap ch'ammo-ch'ongjang | 연합 참모 총장 |
| Army Chief of Staff | yukkun ch'ammo ch'ongjang | 육군 참모 총장 |
| Air Force Chief of Staff | konggun ch'ammo ch'ongjang | 공군 참모 총장 |
| infantry | pobyŏng | 보병 |
| cavalry | kibyŏng | 기병 |
| artillery | p'obyŏng | 포병 |
| engineer | kongbyŏng | 공병 |
| military police | hŏnbyŏng | 헌병 |
| marine corps | haebyŏngdae | 해병대 |
| para-trooper | nak'asanbyŏng | 낙하산병 |
| sniper | chŏgyŏkpyŏng | 저격병 |
| gunner | p'osu | 포수 |
| signalman | shinhobyŏng | 신호병 |
| volunteer | chiwŏnbyŏng | 지원병 |

| | | |
|---|---|---|
| first reserve | yebibyŏng | 예비병 |
| adjutant | pugwan | 부관 |
| guard | poch'o | 보초 |
| cadet | sagwan hubosaeng | 사관 후보생 |
| General Headquarters | ch'ongsaryŏngbu | 총사령부 |
| army | kun | 군 |
| army corps | kundan | 군단 |
| division | sadan | 사단 |
| brigade | yŏdan | 여단 |
| regiment | yŏndae | 연대 |
| battalion | taedae | 대대 |
| company | chungdae | 중대 |
| section | sodae | 소대 |
| squad | pundae | 분대 |
| army corps commander | kundanjang | 군단장 |
| divisional commander | sadanjang | 사단장 |
| regimental commander | yŏndaejang | 연대장 |
| battalion commander | taedaejang | 대대장 |
| company commander | chungdaejang | 중대장 |
| section commander | sodaejang | 소대장 |
| squad leader | pundaejang | 분대장 |
| Military Staff College | yukkundaehak | 육군대학 |
| Naval Staff College | haegundaehak | 해군대학 |
| Military Academy | yukkunsagwan-hakkyo | 육군사관학교 |
| Naval Academy | haegunsagwanhakkyo | 해군사관학교 |
| air base | konggun kiji | 공군 기지 |
| Officers quarters | changgyo sukso | 장교 숙소 |
| G.I. | Migukkunin | 미국 군인 |
| reservist | chaehyang kunin | 재향 군인 |

| | | |
|---|---|---|
| combatant | chŏnt'uwŏn | 전투원 |
| guerilla | yugyŏktae | 유격대 |
| court-martial | kunpŏp hoeŭi | 군법회의 |
| maneuver | kidong yŏnsŭp | 기동 연습 |
| martial law | kyeŏmnyŏng | 계엄령 |
| sortie | ch'ulgyŏk | 출격 |
| decree | p'ogo | 포고 |
| civil war | naeran | 내란 |
| street fighting | shigajŏn | 시가전 |
| naval battle | haejŏn | 해전 |
| cold war | naengjŏn | 냉전 |
| all-out war | chŏnmyŏnjŏn | 전면전 |
| guerilla war | kerillajŏn | 게릴라전 |
| armistice | hyujŏn | 휴전 |
| truce | chŏngjŏn | 정전 |
| emergency | pisang sat'ae | 비상 사태 |
| demilitarized zone | pimujang chidae | 비무장 지대 |
| 38th parallel | samp'alsŏn | 삼팔선 |
| peace line | p'yonghwasŏn | 평화선 |
| off limits | ch'urip kŭmji | 출입 금지 |
| on limits | ch'urip chayu | 출입 자유 |
| curfew | t'onghaeng kŭmjiryŏng | 통행 금지령 |
| martial spirit | sagi | 사기 |
| prisoner of war | p'oro | 포로 |
| puppet regime | koeroe chŏngkwŏn | 괴뢰 정권 |
| purge | sukch'ŏng | 숙청 |
| people's court | inmin chaep'an | 인민 재판 |
| infiltration | ch'imt'u | 침투 |
| sabotage | p'agoe haengwi | 파괴 행위 |
| tank | chŏnch'a | 전차 |

| | | |
|---|---|---|
| mortar | pakkyŏkp'o | 박격포 |
| radar | chŏnp'a t'amjigi | 전파 탐지기 |
| fighter plane | chŏnt'ugi | 전투기 |
| bomber | p'okkyŏkki | 폭격기 |
| reconnaissance plane | chŏngch'algi | 정찰기 |
| jet plane | chet'ŭgi | 제트기 |
| helicopter | hellik'op t'ŏ | 헬리콥터 |
| fleet | hamdae | 함대 |
| warship | kunham | 군함 |
| aircraft carrier | hanggong moham | 항공 모함 |
| destroyer | kuch'uk'am | 구축함 |
| submarine boat | chamsuham | 잠수함 |
| ammunition | t'anyak | 탄약 |
| flare bomb | chomyŏngt'an | 조명탄 |
| hand grenade | suryut'an | 수류탄 |
| cannon ball | p'ot'an | 포탄 |
| bomb | p'okt'an | 폭탄 |
| atomic bomb | wŏnja p'okt'an | 원자 폭탄 |
| H bomb | suso p'okt'an | 수소 폭탄 |
| I. C. B. M | taeryukkan t'andot'an | 대륙간 탄도탄 |
| I. R. B. M | chunggŏri t'andot'an | 중거리 탄도탄 |
| torpedo | ŏroe | 어뢰 |
| mine | chiroe | 지뢰 |
| radioactivity | pangsanŭng | 방사능 |
| artificial satellite | in-gong wisŏng | 인공 위성 |

## LAW

### 법 률(Pŏmnyul)

| | | |
|---|---|---|
| national law | kukkapŏp | 국가법 |

| | | |
|---|---|---|
| constitution | hŏnpŏp | 헌법 |
| administrative law | haengjŏngpŏp | 행정법 |
| public law | kongpŏp | 공법 |
| commercial law | sangpŏp | 상법 |
| proclamation | p'ogo | 포고 |
| ordinance | pŏmnyŏng | 법령 |
| order | myŏngnyŏng | 명령 |
| juristical act | pŏmnyul haengwi | 법률 행위 |
| guardian | hugyŏnin | 후견인 |
| succession | sangsok | 상속 |
| domicile | ponjŏk | 본적 |
| release | myŏnje | 면제 |
| rescission | haeje | 해제 |
| mandate | wiim | 위임 |
| compromise | hwahae | 화해 |
| rights | kwŏlli | 권리 |
| duty | ŭimu | 의무 |
| guaranty fund | pojŭnggŭm | 보증금 |
| personalty | tongsan | 동산 |
| trial | kongp'an | 공판 |
| decision | p'an-gyŏl | 판결 |
| sentence | ŏndo | 언도 |
| condemnation | sŏn-go | 선고 |
| criminal action | koso | 고소 |
| declaration | chinsul | 진술 |
| evidence | chŭnggŏ | 증거 |
| personal rights | inkwŏn | 인권 |
| witness | chŭngin | 증인 |
| natural person | chayŏnin | 자연인 |
| criminal | pŏmin | 범인 |

| | | |
|---|---|---|
| recidinism | sangsŭpchŏk pŏmhaeng | 상습적 범행 |
| recidivist | sangsŭppŏm | 상습범 |
| prisoner | choesu | 죄수 |
| murderer | sarinja | 살인자 |
| burglar | pamtoduk | 밤도둑 |
| conspiracy | kongmo | 공모 |
| criminal connection | kant'ong | 간통 |
| arrest | ch'ep'o | 체포 |
| detention | kuryu | 구류 |
| penal servitude | chingyŏk | 징역 |
| imprisonment | kŭmgo(t'uok) | 금고(투옥) |
| bail | posŏk | 보석 |
| police fine | pŏlgŭm | 벌금 |

# APPENDIX I

## ANNUAL EVENTS IN KOREA
## 한국의 연중 행사(Han-gugŭi Yŏnjung Haengsa)

| | | |
|---|---|---|
| New Year's Day | Sŏllal | 설날 |
| March 1 Independence Movement Day | Samilchŏl | 삼일절 |
| Arbor Day | Shingmogil | 식목일 |
| Children's Day | Ŏrininal | 어린이날 |
| Buddha's Birthday | Sŏkka t'anshinil | 석가 탄신일 |
| Parents' Day | Ŏbŏinal | 어버이날 |
| Memorial Day | Hyŏnch'ungil | 현충일 |
| Constitution Day | Chehŏnjŏl | 제헌절 |
| Liberation Day | Kwangbokchŏl | 광복절 |
| Moon Festival | Ch'usŏk | 추석 |
| Armed Forces Day | Kukkunŭi nal | 국군의 날 |
| National Foundation Day | Kaech'ŏnjŏl | 개천절 |
| Korean Letter Day | Han-gŭllal | 한글날 |
| Christmas | Sŏngt'anjŏl | 성탄절 |

## POSTED SIGNS
## 게시 용어(Keshi Yongŏ)

| | | |
|---|---|---|
| Bus Stop | Pŏsŭchŏngnyujang | 버스 정류장 |
| Caution | Chuŭi | 주의 |
| Closed | Hyuŏp | 휴업 |
| Danger | Wihŏm | 위험 |
| Engaged | Sayongjung | 사용중 |
| Entrance | Ipku | 입구 |
| Exit | Ch'ulgu | 출구 |
| Fire Caution | Puljoshim | 불조심 |

| | | |
|---|---|---|
| For Information | Annae | 안내 |
| Go Slow | Sŏhaeng | 서행 |
| Hands Off | Sondaeji mashio | 손대지 마시오 |
| Keep Off The Grass | Chandie tŭrŏgaji mashio | 잔디에 들어가지 마시오 |
| Keep Out | Tŭrŏgaji mashio | 들어가지 마시오 |
| No Admission | Ipchang purhŏ | 입장 불허 |
| No Left Turn | Chwahoejŏn kŭmji | 좌회전 금지 |
| No Parking | Chuch'a kŭmji | 주차 금지 |
| No Smoking | Kŭmyŏn | 금연 |
| On Sale | P'anmaejung | 판매중 |
| Please Wipe Your Feet | Shinbarŭl takkŭshio | 신발을 닦으시오 |
| Pull | Tanggishio | 당기시오 |
| Push | Mishio | 미시오 |
| Road Closed | T'onghaeng kŭmji | 통행 금지 |
| Slow | Ch'ŏnch'ŏnhi | 천천히 |
| Speed Limit | Sokto chehan | 속도 제한 |
| Stop | Chŏngji | 정지 |
| Under Repair | Surijung | 수리중 |
| Warning | Kyŏnggo | 경고 |
| Welcome | Hwanyŏng | 환영 |
| Wet Paint | Ch'il chuŭi | 칠 주의 |

## ADMINISTRATIVE UNITS IN KOREA
## 한국의 행정 구역 지명
## (Han-gugŭi Haengjŏng Kuyŏk Chimyŏng)

| | |
|---|---|
| Kyŏnggi-do | 경기도 |
| Kangwŏn-do | 강원도 |
| Ch'ungch'ŏng-buk-do | 충청북도 |
| Ch'ungch'ŏng-nam-do | 충청남도 |
| Chŏllabuk-do | 전라북도 |
| Chŏllanam-do | 전라남도 |

| | | | |
|---|---|---|---|
| Kyŏngsangbuk-do | 경상북도 | Chŏnju | 전주 |
| | | Kunsan | 군산 |
| Kyŏngsangnam-do | 경상남도 | Iri | 이리 |
| | | Kwangju | 광주 |
| Cheju-do | 제주도 | Mokp'o | 목포 |
| Seoul | 서울 | Yŏsu | 여수 |
| Pusan | 부산 | Sunch'ŏn | 순천 |
| Taegu | 대구 | P'ohang | 포항 |
| Inch'ŏn | 인천 | Kyŏngju | 경주 |
| Kimp'o | 김포 | Kimch'ŏn | 김천 |
| Suwŏn | 수원 | Andong | 안동 |
| Ŭijŏngbu | 의정부 | Kumi | 구미 |
| Anyang | 안양 | Masan | 마산 |
| Tongduch'ŏn | 동두천 | Ulsan | 울산 |
| Ch'unch'ŏn | 춘천 | Chinju | 진주 |
| Wŏnju | 원주 | Ch'angwŏn | 창원 |
| Kangnŭng | 강릉 | Chinhae | 진해 |
| Sokch'o | 속초 | Ch'ungmu | 충무 |
| Ch'ŏngju | 청주 | Samch'ŏnp'o | 삼천포 |
| Ch'ungju | 충주 | Kimhae | 김해 |
| Taejŏn | 대전 | Cheju | 제주 |
| Ch'ŏnan | 천안 | Sŏgwip'o | 서귀포 |

## STORE SIGNS
간판(Kanp'an)

| | | |
|---|---|---|
| Drugstore | Yakkuk | 약국 |
| Cigar | Tambae | 담배 |
| Tearoom | Tabang, Tashil | 다방, 다실 |
| Public Phone | Kongjung chŏnhwa | 공중 전화 |
| Furniture Shop | Kagujŏm | 가구점 |

| | | |
|---|---|---|
| Real Estate Agency | Pudongsan, Poktŏkpang | 부동산, 복덕방 |
| Hospital | Pyŏngwŏn | 병원 |
| Grocery | Shikp'umjŏm | 식품점 |
| Restaurant | Ŭmshikchŏm, Shiktang | 음식점, 식당 |
| Tailor's Shop | Yangbokchŏm | 양복점 |
| Dressmaking Shop | Yangjangjŏm | 양장점 |
| Haberdashery | Yangp'umjŏm | 양품점 |
| Bank | Ŭnhaeng | 은행 |
| Bakery | Chegwajŏm | 제과점 |
| Inn | Yŏgwan | 여관 |
| Bookstore | Sŏjŏm, Ch'aekpang | 서점, 책방 |

## SURNAMES OF KOREANS
### 한국인의 성(Han-guginŭi Sŏng)

| Surname | Korean | Chinese |
|---|---|---|
| Kim | 김 | 金 |
| Lee, Yi | 이 | 李 |
| Park | 박 | 朴 |
| Chŏng | 정 | 鄭 |
| Yun | 윤 | 尹 |
| Ch'oe | 최 | 崔 |
| Ryu | 유 | 柳 |
| Hong | 홍 | 洪 |
| Shin | 신 | 申 |
| Kwŏn | 권 | 權 |
| Cho | 조 | 趙 |
| Han | 한 | 韓 |
| Oh | 오 | 吳 |
| Kang | 강 | 姜 |
| Shim | 심 | 沈 |

| Surname | Korean | Chinese |
|---|---|---|
| An | 안 | 安 |
| Hŏ | 허 | 許 |
| Chang | 장 | 張 |
| Min | 민 | 閔 |
| Im | 임 | 任 |
| Rim | 임 | 林 |
| Nam | 남 | 南 |
| Sŏ | 서 | 徐 |
| Ku | 구 | 具 |
| Sŏng | 성 | 成 |
| Song | 송 | 宋 |
| Yu | 유 | 兪 |
| Wŏn | 원 | 元 |
| Hwang | 황 | 黃 |
| Cho | 조 | 曺 |
| Yŏ | 여 | 呂 |
| Yang | 양 | 梁 |
| Chu | 주 | 朱 |
| Yu | 유 | 劉 |
| Na | 나 | 羅 |
| Kang | 강 | 康 |
| Ko | 고 | 高 |
| Chŏng | 정 | 丁 |
| Ham | 함 | 咸 |
| No | 노 | 盧 |

* There are about 200 Korean surnames, but of these, Kim, Lee and Park are the names of more than half the population. Above-mentioned surnames are the other common names.

# APPENDIX II

## *TO HELP YOU UNDERSTAND KOREAN ALPHABET AND SOME WRITINGS IN KOREAN*

# 1. Romanization of the Korean Alphabet
(Based on the Ministry of Education System)

## 1. *Vowels*

| ㅏ | ㅑ | ㅓ | ㅕ | ㅗ | ㅛ | ㅜ | ㅠ |
|---|---|---|---|---|---|---|---|
| a | ya | ŏ | yŏ | o | yo | u | yu |
| ㅡ | ㅣ | ㅐ | ㅒ | ㅔ | ㅖ | ㅚ | ㅟ |
| ŭ | i | ae | yae | e | ye | oe | wi |
| ㅢ | ㅘ | ㅙ | ㅝ | ㅞ | | | |
| ŭi | wa | wae | wŏ | we | | | |

## 2. *Consonants*

| ㄱ | ㄴ | ㄷ | ㄹ | ㅁ | ㅂ | ㅅ | ㅇ |
|---|---|---|---|---|---|---|---|
| k(g) | n | t(d) | r(l) | m | p(b) | s | ng |
| ㅈ | ㅊ | ㅋ | ㅌ | ㅍ | ㅎ | ㄲ | ㄸ |
| ch(j) | ch' | k' | t' | p' | h | kk | tt |
| ㅃ | ㅆ | ㅉ | | | | | |
| pp | ss | tch | | | | | |

## 3. *Syllabary*

| 가 | 갸 | 거 | 겨 | 고 | 교 | 구 | 규 |
|---|---|---|---|---|---|---|---|
| k(g)a | kya | kŏ | kyŏ | ko | kyo | ku | kyu |
| 그 | 기 | 개 | 걔 | 게 | 계 | 괴 | 귀 |
| kŭ | ki | kae | kyae | ke | kye | koe | kwi |
| 긔 | 과 | 괘 | 궈 | 궤 | | | |
| kŭi | kwa | kwae | kwŏ | kwe | | | |

| 나 | 냐 | 너 | 녀 | 노 | 뇨 | 누 | 뉴 |
|---|---|---|---|---|---|---|---|
| na | nya | nŏ | nyŏ | no | nyo | nu | nyu |
| 느 | 니 | 내 | 냬 | 네 | 녜 | 뇌 | 뉘 |
| nŭ | ni | nae | nyae | ne | nye | noe | nwi |
| 늬 | 놔 | 놰 | 눠 | 눼 | | | |
| nŭi | nwa | nwae | nwŏ | nwe | | | |
| 다 | 댜 | 더 | 뎌 | 도 | 됴 | 두 | 듀 |
| t(d)a | tya | tŏ | tyŏ | to | tyo | tu | tyu |
| 드 | 디 | 대 | 댸 | 데 | 뎨 | 되 | 뒤 |
| tŭ | ti | tae | tyae | te | tye | toe | twi |
| 듸 | 돠 | 돼 | 둬 | 뒈 | | | |
| tŭi | twa | twae | twŏ | twe | | | |
| 라 | 랴 | 러 | 려 | 로 | 료 | 루 | 류 |
| r(l)a | rya | rŏ | ryŏ | ro | ryo | ru | ryu |
| 르 | 리 | 래 | 럐 | 레 | 례 | 뢰 | 뤼 |
| rŭ | ri | rae | rya | re | rye | roe | rwi |
| 릐 | 롸 | 뢔 | 뤄 | 뤠 | | | |
| rŭi | rwa | rwae | rwŏ | rwe | | | |
| 마 | 먀 | 머 | 며 | 모 | 묘 | 무 | 뮤 |
| ma | mya | mŏ | myŏ | mo | myo | mu | myu |
| 므 | 미 | 매 | 먜 | 메 | 몌 | 뫼 | 뮈 |
| mŭ | mi | mae | myae | me | mye | moe | mwi |
| 믜 | 뫄 | 뫠 | 뭐 | 뭬 | | | |
| mŭi | mwa | mwae | mwŏ | mwe | | | |
| 바 | 뱌 | 버 | 벼 | 보 | 뵤 | 부 | 뷰 |
| p(b)a | pya | pŏ | pyŏ | po | pyo | pu | pyu |
| 브 | 비 | 배 | 뱨 | 베 | 볘 | 뵈 | 뷔 |
| pŭ | pi | pae | pyae | pe | pye | poe | pwi |
| 븨 | 봐 | 봬 | 붜 | 붸 | | | |
| pŭi | pwa | pwae | pwŏ | pwe | | | |
| 사 | 샤 | 서 | 셔 | 소 | 쇼 | 수 | 슈 |
| sa | sya | sŏ | syŏ | so | syo | su | syu |
| 스 | 시 | 새 | 섀 | 세 | 셰 | 쇠 | 쉬 |
| sŭ | shi | sae | syae | se | sye | soe | shwi |

| 싀 | 솨 | 쇄 | 숴 | 쉐 | | | |
|---|---|---|---|---|---|---|---|
| sŭi | swa | swae | swŏ | swe | | | |
| 아 | 야 | 어 | 여 | 오 | 요 | 우 | 유 |
| a | ya | ŏ | yŏ | o | yo | u | yu |
| 으 | 이 | 애 | 얘 | 에 | 예 | 외 | 위 |
| ŭ | i | ae | yae | e | ye | oe | wi |
| 의 | 와 | 왜 | 워 | 웨 | | | |
| ŭi | wa | wae | wŏ | we | | | |
| 자 | 쟈 | 저 | 져 | 조 | 죠 | 주 | 쥬 |
| ch(j)a | chya | chŏ | chyŏ | cho | chyo | chu | chyu |
| 즈 | 지 | 재 | 쟤 | 제 | 졔 | 죄 | 쥐 |
| chŭ | chi | chae | chyae | che | chye | choe | chwi |
| 즤 | 좌 | 좨 | 줘 | 줴 | | | |
| chŭi | chwa | chwae | chwŏ | chwe | | | |
| 차 | 챠 | 처 | 쳐 | 초 | 쵸 | 추 | 츄 |
| ch'a | ch'ya | ch'ŏ | ch'yŏ | ch'o | ch'yo | ch'u | ch'yu |
| 츠 | 치 | 채 | 챼 | 체 | 쳬 | 최 | 취 |
| ch'ŭ | ch'i | ch'ae | ch'yae | ch'e | ch'ye | ch'oe | ch'wi |
| 츼 | 촤 | 쵀 | 춰 | 췌 | | | |
| ch'ŭi | ch'wa | ch'wae | ch'wŏ | ch'we | | | |
| 카 | 캬 | 커 | 켜 | 코 | 쿄 | 쿠 | 큐 |
| k'a | k'ya | k'ŏ | k'yŏ | k'o | k'yo | k'u | k'yu |
| 크 | 키 | 캐 | 컈 | 케 | 켸 | 쾨 | 퀴 |
| k'ŭ | k'i | k'ae | k'yae | k'e | k'ye | k'oe | k'wi |
| 킈 | 콰 | 쾌 | 쿼 | 퀘 | | | |
| k'ŭi | k'wa | k'wae | k'wŏ | k'we | | | |
| 타 | 탸 | 터 | 텨 | 토 | 툐 | 투 | 튜 |
| t'a | t'ya | t'ŏ | t'yŏ | t'o | t'yo | t'u | t'yu |
| 트 | 티 | 태 | 턔 | 테 | 톄 | 퇴 | 튀 |
| t'ŭ | t'i | t'ae | t'yae | t'e | t'ye | t'oe | t'wi |
| 틔 | 톼 | 퇘 | 퉈 | 퉤 | | | |
| t'ŭi | t'wa | t'wae | t'wŏ | t'we | | | |
| 파 | 퍄 | 퍼 | 펴 | 포 | 표 | 푸 | 퓨 |
| p'a | p'ya | p'ŏ | p'yŏ | p'o | p'yo | p'u | p'yu |

| 프 | 피 | 패 | 퍠 | 페 | 폐 | 푀 | 퓌 |
|---|---|---|---|---|---|---|---|
| p'ŭ | p'i | p'ae | p'yae | p'e | p'ye | p'oe | p'wi |
| 픠 | 퐈 | 퐤 | 풔 | 풰 | | | |
| p'ŭi | p'wa | p'wae | p'wŏ | p'we | | | |
| 하 | 햐 | 허 | 혀 | 호 | 효 | 후 | 휴 |
| ha | hya | hŏ | hyŏ | ho | hyo | hu | hyu |
| 흐 | 히 | 해 | 햬 | 헤 | 혜 | 회 | 휘 |
| hŭ | hi | hae | hyae | he | hye | hoe | hwi |
| 희 | 화 | 홰 | 훠 | 훼 | | | |
| hŭi | hwa | hwae | hwŏ | hwe | | | |

## 2. The Korean Alphabet and Pronunciation

The Korean Alphabet, Hun Min Chŏng Ŭm (훈민정음) was invented by King Sejong of the Yi Dynasty more than five centuries ago.

There are 21 vowels and 19 consonants provided under the structure of the Korean Alphabet of 24 letters, 14 consonants and 10 vowels.

Vowels: ㅏ ㅑ ㅓ ㅕ ㅗ ㅛ ㅜ ㅠ ㅡ ㅣ ㅐ ㅔ ㅚ ㅢ ㅝ ㅞ ㅒ ㅖ ㅟ ㅘ ㅙ

Consonants: ㄱ ㄴ ㄷ ㄹ ㅁ ㅂ ㅅ ㅇ ㅈ ㅊ ㅋ ㅌ ㅍ ㅎ ㄲ ㄸ ㅃ ㅆ ㅉ

### 1. *Vowel Sounds*

The vowels of the Korean Alphabet are classified in the writing form into two categories, simple and compound.

The English sounds given here are, of course, approximate ones.

| Simple Vowels | | | |
|---|---|---|---|
| Korean | English Sounds | Korean | English Sounds |
| 아 a | as ah | 야 ya | as yard |
| 어 ŏ | approximately as saw | 여 yŏ | approximately yearn |
| 오 o | as oh | 요 yo | as yoke |
| 우 u | as do | 유 yu | as you |
| 으 ŭ | approximately taken | | |
| 이 i | as ink | | |

| Compound Vowels | | | |
|---|---|---|---|
| Korean | English Sounds | Korean | English Sounds |
| 애 ae | as at | 얘 yae | as yam |
| 에 e | as met | 예 ye | as yes |
| 외 oe | as Köln | 위 wi | as we |
| 의 ŭi | approximately taken+we | 와 wa | as wander |
| 워 wŏ | as water | 왜 wae | as WAC |
| 웨 we | as wet | | |

"ㅇ" in the above table is classified under consonants, but it is silent at the beginning of a letter.

## *2. Consonant Sounds*

### 1. Simple Consonants

| Korean | English Sounds | Korean | English Sounds |
|---|---|---|---|
| ㄱ<br>k/g | k or g<br>as king or grocer<br>(lightly aspirated) | ㄴ<br>n | n<br>as name |
| ㄷ<br>t/d | t or d<br>as toy or depend<br>(lightly aspirated) | ㄹ<br>r/l | r or l<br>as rain or lily |
| ㅁ<br>m | m<br>as mother | ㅂ<br>p/b | p or b<br>as pin or book<br>(lightly aspirated) |
| ㅅ<br>s/sh | s<br>as same<br>(lightly pronounced) | ㅇ<br>o | o or ng<br>as ah or king |
| ㅈ<br>ch/j | j<br>as John | ㅊ<br>ch' | ch<br>as church |
| ㅋ<br>k' | k<br>as kate | ㅌ<br>t' | t<br>as tank |
| ㅍ<br>p' | p<br>as pump | ㅎ<br>h | h<br>as high |

There are no f's, v's and z's in Korean sounds.

### 2. Double Consonants

*a. For initial or final positions*

These are pronounced stronger than single counterpart.

| Korean | English Sounds | Korean | English Sounds |
|---|---|---|---|
| ㄲ<br>kk | (kk) as sky or Jack | ㄸ<br>tt | (tt) as stay |
| ㅃ<br>pp | (pp) as spy | ㅆ<br>ss | (ss) as essence. |
| ㅉ<br>tch | (tch) as joy with a strong emphasis | | |

*b. For final positions only*

These consonants will have full sound values depending on the word that follows.

| Korean | English Sounds | Korean | English Sounds |
|---|---|---|---|
| ㄳ | ks<br>Ex. 넋 | ㄵ | nj<br>Ex. 앉다 |
| ㄶ | nh<br>Ex. 많다 | ㄺ | lk<br>Ex. 읽다 |
| ㄻ | lm<br>Ex. 삶다 | ㄼ | lb<br>Ex. 얇다 |
| ㄾ | rt<br>Ex. 핥다 | ㄿ | lp'<br>Ex. 읊다 |
| ㅀ | lh<br>Ex. 싫다 | ㅄ | ps<br>Ex. 값 |

## 3. Sound Changes

Some sound changes take place when the words are linked together.

The following table will give you a convenient guideline.

| Final / Initial | | ㄱ | ㄴ | ㄹ | ㅁ | ㅂ | ㅇ |
|---|---|---|---|---|---|---|---|
| | | k | n | l | m | p | ng |
| ㅇ | | g | n | r | m | b | ng |
| ㄱ | k | kk | n-g(k) | lg(k) | mg | pk | ngg(k) |
| ㄴ | n | ngn | nn | ll | mn | mn | ngn |
| ㄷ | t | kt | nd(t) | lt(d) | md(t) | pt | ngd(t) |
| ㄹ | (r) | ngn | ll | ll | mn | mn | ngn |
| ㅁ | m | ngm | nm | lm | mm | mm | ngm |
| ㅂ | p | kp | nb(p) | lb(p) | mb(p) | pp | ngb(p) |
| ㅅ | s | ks | ns | ls | ms | ps | ngs |
| ㅈ | ch | kch | nj(ch) | lj(ch) | mj(ch) | pch | ngj(ch) |
| ㅊ | ch' | kch' | nch' | lch' | mch' | pch' | ngch' |
| ㅋ | k' | kk' | nk' | lk' | mk' | pk' | ngk' |
| ㅌ | t' | kt' | nt' | lt' | mt' | pt' | ngt' |
| ㅍ | p' | kp' | np' | lp' | mp' | pp' | ngp' |
| ㅎ | h | kh | nh | rh | mb | ph | ngh |

Adopted from the simplified table by McCune-Reischauer.

## 4. *Rule to Form a Syllable*

The Korean Alphabet is not used the like English Alphabet. The Korean Alphabet is used to build up separate syllables.

For example, ㄱ + ㅏ = 가, ㄱ + ㅏ + ㅁ = 감
k a ka k a m kam

**The general rule is:**

Consonant or Silent "ㅇ" + Vowel + Consonant

**More examples:**

| Korean Letter Complete Syllable | Initial Consonant | Vowel | Consonant | Pronounced |
|---|---|---|---|---|
| 아 | ㅇ (Silent) | ㅏ | none | ah |
| 너 | ㄴ | ㅓ | none | as nonsense |
| 씨 | ㅆ | ㅣ | none | as seat |
| 산 | ㅅ | ㅏ | ㄴ | san |
| 흙 | ㅎ | ㅡ | ㄺ | hŭk |
| 땅 | ㄸ | ㅏ | ㅇ | ttang |
| 꿩 | ㄲ | ㅝ | ㅇ | kkwŏng |

## 5. *Table of Pronouns*

| English | Korean |
|---|---|
| I | nanŭn(*or* naega) |
| We | urinŭn(*or* uriga) |
| My | naŭi |

| | |
|---|---|
| Our | uriŭi |
| Me | na-ege(*or* narŭl) |
| Us | uriege(*or* urirŭl) |
| You | tangshinŭn(*or* tangshini) |
| Your | tangshinŭi |
| You | tangshinege(tangshinŭl) |
| He | kŭnŭn(*or* kŭga) |
| His | kŭŭi |
| Him | kŭrŭl(*or* kŭege) |
| She | kŭ yŏjaga(*or* kŭ yŏjanŭn) |
| Her | kŭ yŏjaŭi |
| Her | kŭ yŏjarŭl(*or* kŭ yŏja-ege) |
| They | kŭdŭrŭn(*or* kŭdŭri) |
| Their | kŭdŭrŭi |
| Them | kŭdŭrege(*or* kŭdŭrŭl) |

## 3. How to Write the Words in *Han-gŭl*, the Korean Alphabet

Unlike in English, *Han-gŭl*, the Korean alphabet, does not have different types of writing in printing or in long hand. Also unlike in English, there are no capital letters, nor are there small letters. Although English can be written only horizontally from left to right, the *Han-gŭl* could be written vertically from up to down as well as horizontally, usually from left to right.

# 1. How to write Korean Alphabet, *Han-gul*

| 가(ka) | 나(na) | 다(ta) | 라(ra) | 마(ma) |
|---|---|---|---|---|
| ① ② 가 ③ | ① 나 | ① ② 다 | ① ② ③ 라 | ① ② 마 ③ |

| 바(pa) | 사(sa) | 아(a) | 자(cha) | 차(ch'a) |
|---|---|---|---|---|
| ② ③ ① 바 ④ | ① 사 ② | ① 아 | ① 자 ② | ① ② 차 ③ |

| 카(k'a) | 타(t'a) | 파(p'a) | 하(ha) | |
|---|---|---|---|---|
| ① ② 카 | ① ② ③ 타 | ① ③ ② 파 ④ | ① ② ③ 하 | |

## 2. Some words

| | | |
|---|---|---|
| 감자<br>[kamja]<br>(Potato) | 나비<br>[nabi]<br>(Butterfly) | 담배<br>[tambae]<br>(Tobacco) |
| 라디오<br>[radio]<br>(Radio) | 마음<br>[maŭm]<br>(Heart) | 바람<br>[param]<br>(Wind) |
| 사과<br>[sagwa]<br>(Apple) | 안개<br>[an-gae]<br>(Fog) | 자동차<br>[chadongch'a]<br>(Car) |
| 책상<br>[ch'aeksang]<br>(Desk) | 칼<br>[k'al]<br>(Knife) | 탁구<br>[t'akku]<br>(Ping-pong) |
| 팔<br>[p'al]<br>(Arm) | 학생<br>[haksaeng]<br>(Pupil) | |

## 3. Composition

안녕하십니까?

[Annyŏnghashimnikka?]
(Good morning.)

대단히 고맙습니다.

[Taedanhi komapsŭmnida.]
(Thank you very much.)

미안합니다.

[Mianhamnida.]
(I am sorry.)

어서 들어오십시오.

[Ŏsŏ tŭrŏoshipshio.]
(Please come in.)

앉으십시오.

[Anjŭshipshio.]
(Sit down, please.)

## 4. A few examples of notes and messages

미스 김에게

조그만 선물을 보내 드립니다. 마음에 드실지 모르겠읍니다.

1999년 1월 5일
호레이스 브라운

January 5, 1999

Dear Miss Kim,

I am sending you a small gift. I hope you will like it.

As always,
Horace Brown

5월 7일 화요일 11시 뉴요크 성토
마스 교회에서 여식 제인과 도널드 웨
인의 결혼식을 거행하겠사오니 참석하
여 주시기 바랍니다.

조오지 콜맨 부처

Mr. and Mrs. George Coleman
request the honor of your presence
at the marriage of their daughter
Jane
to
Mr. Donald Wayne
on Tuesday morning, the seventh of May
at eleven o'clock
St. Thomas Church
New York

Sincerely,
Mr. & Mrs. George Coleman

웨이드 부인께

부인께서 병환이라는 소식을 듣고 대단히 유감스러웠읍니다. 빨리 완쾌하시리라 믿고 있읍니다. 이웃 사람들은 모두 부인이 안 계셔서 섭섭해 하고 있읍니다. 부인께서 곧 회복하시기를 빕니다.

수잔 제닝스

Dear Mrs. Wade,

I was so sorry to learn of your illness. You must hurry and get well! Everybody in the neighborhood misses you, and we're all hoping you'll be back soon.

Sincerely yours.
Susan Jennings

정 선생님 내외분께

1월 18일 토요일은 저의 처 생일입니다. 오후 7시에 저의 집에서 저녁식사를 두분과 함께 할까 합니다. 와주시면 대단히 영광이겠읍니다.

1999년 1월 5일

존 노웰 부처

---

January 5, 1999

Dear Mr. & Mrs. Chung,

It will give me much pleasure if you will come to dinner at my house on Saturday, January 18th(at seven P. M.), for your information the day is my wife's birthday.

Sincerely,
Mr. & Mrs. John Nowell

즐거운 성탄을 경축하오며
새해에 복 많이 받으시기 바랍니다.

조오지 김

Best Wishes for
A Merry Christmas and
A Happy New Year

George Kim

HEART OF SEOUL
Sejong Cultural Center
SEJONG-RO
Independence Arch
Australian Embassy
Koreana Hotel
City Hall
Seoul Foreign School
Red Cross Hospital
British Embassy
German Embassy
Yonsei Univ
Yonsei Univ Hospital
Plaza Hotel
Tongbang Bldg
Bank of Korea
Ewha Woman's Univ
French Embassy
#2 SUBWAY
South Gate
SŎNGSAN BRIDGE
Sŏgang Univ
Daewoo Bldg
Seoul Railroad Station
Hongik Univ
YANGHWA BRIDGE
Kimp'o Airport
Hyoch'ang Stadium
Sungmyŏng Woman's Univ
Seoul Garden Hotel
National Assembly
KBS
MAP'O BRIDGE
YŎŬI-DO
MBC
WONHYO BRIDGE
Yongsan Station
Shindorim Station
Taehan Life Insurance Bldg
HAN RIVER
Yŏngdŭngp'o Station
Noryangjin Station
HAN-GANG BRIDGE